MICKEY LAWLER'S
SKYDYES
A VISUAL GUIDE TO FABRIC PAINTING

I owe the beauty of this book
mostly to the enormous talent of my friend and
photographer Jack McConnell.

MICKEY LAWLER'S
SKYDYES

A VISUAL GUIDE TO FABRIC PAINTING

C&T PUBLISHING

Editor: Annie Nelson

Technical Editor: Lynn Koolish

Book Design: Rose Sheifer

Cover Design: Christina Jarumay

Graphic Illustrations: Lynn Koolish

Photography: Jack McConnell and McConnell McNamara, Wethersfield, Connecticut, unless otherwise noted.

Photos on page 31: Bruce R. Wright

Attention Teachers:

C&T Publishing, Inc. encourages you to use this book as a text for teaching. Contact us at 800-284-1114 or www.ctpub.com for more information about the C&T Teachers Program.

Excerpt on page 11 reprinted from *Writing From the Heart: Tapping the Power of Your Inner Voice* by Nancy Slonim Aronie. Copyright © 1998 by Nancy Slonim Aronie. Published by Hyperion.

Library of Congress Cataloging-in-Publication Data

Lawler, Mickey.
Skydyes : a visual guide to fabric painting / Mickey Lawler.
p.   cm.
Includes bibliographical references and index.
ISBN 1-57120-072-X (pbk.)
1. Textile painting. 2. Skies in art. 3. Patchwork quilts.
I. Title.   II. Skydyes

TT851 .L39 1999   98-58154
  746.6—dc21   CIP

Published by C&T Publishing, Inc.
P.O. Box 1456
Lafayette, California 94549

Printed in Hong Kong
10 9 8 7 6 5 4 3 2 1

TABLE OF CONTENTS

In Gratitude

I must tell you that I have thoroughly enjoyed working on this book and am sincerely grateful to Todd Hensley of C&T Publishing for the opportunity  to see it in print. Many thanks also go to my editor, Annie Nelson, and to Production Director Diane Pedersen, who were always enthusiastic and encouraging. It was great to work with all of you.

I owe the beauty of this book mostly to the enormous talent of my friend and photographer Jack McConnell of McConnell McNamara, Wethersfield, Connecticut. Thanks, Jack, for your patience, expertise, skill, creativity, and to you and Paula both for making our "shoots" fun as well.

I also wish to thank Judy Smith-Kressley for photographing many of the quilts featured in the following pages. It was a pleasure to know I could entrust these quilts to you.

To each of the artists who so generously and graciously shared their work for inclusion in this book, I am truly grateful.

Since I have this opportunity, it gives me great pleasure to publicly acknowledge a few other people who have been important to me along the road I've travelled…

Thanks first are due to my old friend Ann Luby, whose meticulous and unflinching care in heatsetting and pressing literally thousands of yards of Skydyes fabric over the years is, and will forever be, unequaled. Where would we be without you?

I am especially grateful to Michael James and Judi Warren for their passionate and enduring contributions to the aesthetic development of quiltmaking—and for sharing it all!

Margy Brehmer, thank you, my friend and mentor. You have, with your grace and humor, through your poetry, and in person, constantly been my lamp, lighting the path ahead.

My thanks go to Jean Thibodeau and Pam Hardiman for their courage and vision in providing New England quilters with the vital, inspiring, and out-of-the-ordinary Double T Quilt Shop of Springfield, Massachusetts, since 1978. I bought my first bottles of fabric paint from them!

I will be forever grateful to the early Quilters Connection group in the Boston area which included Nancy Halpern, Sue Turbak, Ruth McDowell, Rhoda Cohen, and so many others who influenced and excited us as new quilters in the 70s and 80s and continue to do so today.

I am especially indebted to Jean Ray Laury for writing The Creative Woman's Getting-It-All-Together-At-Home Handbook at a time when I—and thousands of others—needed to hear what she generously and graciously presented.

Thanks also are due to the tireless organizers of quilt symposia and shows who give us all a place to come together, to learn, to excel, and to simply enjoy each other's company.

My good and dear friends, Holly Becket, Ed and Marlene Mayes, Abbie Hodges, Barbara Wysocki, and Judy Robbins, thank you.

There is no way to thank, personally, each of you, students and customers who, through many years, have encouraged and supported my work. Each picture you send of finished projects using fabric I have painted, each comment about how a piece of fabric inspires you, has touched me and given me renewed energy.

Thank you all.

Dedication

I dedicate this book and the present culmination of many years of work to my loving and nourishing family.

First, to my cherished lifelong partner and husband, Dan, who has provided me with a sheltered port from which to sail.

Also to our three grown daughters, Mary, Terry, and Kate, who have made the voyage rich with waves of laughter amid all kinds of weather.

Last, to my beautiful mother, Mary Kirk Doyle Carson, whose indefatigable optimism during her 93 years of life has had a deep and lasting influence on all that I am.

I will always be profoundly grateful.

Detail of *Sails*

Introduction

There are really only two things you need to remember to successfully complete the paintings in this book, and you probably learned these by the first grade:

64 crayons are more fun than 8

and

Recess is the best part of the day!

Neither has to do with that unfortunate word, "talent," or, for that matter, your experience as a painter. What is required is that you simply suspend any desire for total control, accept a playful attitude toward your work, and allow a sense of awe to be your daily companion. You probably already recognize the signs: the clock becomes irrelevant, and a span of fifty lifetimes doesn't seem long enough to pursue all the ideas that come to mind.

This book is intended for beginning fabric painters and those who have already dabbled with paints on fabric. It is meant for those who don't want to limit themselves to current trends of color choices available commercially. This book is by no means the last word on the subject; it is simply encouragement and instruction to try my style of painting. It is also my hope you will have as much fun as I do when creating your own fabrics. Certainly, I understand your desire to learn to mix colors and apply paint; that will come with hands-on practice. Be assured that the more time you spend painting, the more you will learn. That cannot help happening. What is far more important, however, is your involvement in the process—the enjoyable pursuit of color and paint, the point at which fifty lifetimes really can exist in one.

> What is required is that you simply suspend any desire for total control, accept a playful attitude toward your work, and allow a sense of awe to be your daily companion.

By the early 1980s, I had made quilts for over ten years. We quiltmakers who had ventured into abstract and realistic landscape quilts found ourselves desperate for good sky fabric. Using the backs of blue and white flower prints or bleaching streaks in solid blue, we hoped that, from a distance, these fabrics would "read" as sky. A few blue tie-dyes emerged from a major fabric company only to be discontinued within six months. But this was enough to make me realize that I could create my own skies. At first I dyed white cotton but soon discovered fabric paints. Using paints instead of dyes gave me greater freedom. Here I found no heavy pots, no toxic worries, no measuring or fuss—just the pure enjoyment of color on fabric.

Sails, 58"x 47", 1992

Sails was the first quilt I
designed using predominant-
ly hand-painted fabrics. I
generally don't paint fabric
to fit a preconceived idea—
but rather—I allow the fabrics
to inspire the design.

Learn from many different sources. Let the experiences and the instructions of others filter through you until little particles here and there are caught and merge into something that feels just right for you.

Learn from many different sources. Let the experiences and the instructions of others filter through you until little particles here and there are caught and merge into something that feels just right for you. There are those who intentionally, and unintentionally, have much to teach us. Let me tell you of an experience.

In the mid-70s I was working part-time in a small fabric store. I had been making quilts for about six years, and teaching quiltmaking to 35 students a semester through an adult education class for about four years. Obviously, my students and I were learning together.

One day a woman came into the store and asked, rather imperiously, where she might find good cottons to make quilts. I no longer recall her name or what she looked like. I must have noticed her hands more than her face because I can remember only well-manicured nails and three large dinner rings. Now, at that time, it wasn't common to run into another quilter, so, thinking we had an immediate bond, I must have acted like a friendly puppy when I excitedly announced that I was a quilter also. She backed up a step, straightened, and informed me that she was an "expert" quiltmaker and taught small classes in the area. Something in me didn't want to pursue the conversation, so I directed her to the cottons, transacted her sale, and she left.

A few months later, two young women looking for dressmaker fabrics came into the store. We chatted, and the subject of quilts came up. They glanced at each other, rolled their eyes, and stated in no uncertain terms that they would never make a quilt. It seems they had taken a class from the "Self-Proclaimed Expert." They had spent eight weeks working on one block, cutting, sewing, and ripping, over and over, never quite to the teacher's satisfaction, ad nauseam, until their blocks and their enthusiasm were in tatters. I count all three women among my teachers and have since tried to avoid self-proclaimed experts.

My high school friend Nancy Slonim Aronie, a writer and teacher of writing, states, "The label thing is dangerous, because when you think you're a 'whatever-your-label-is,' then you have to be a 'whatever' expert. And when you're an expert, there's no room for error. There's no chance for discovery. There's no 'anything-is-possible' because the expert has explored all the possibilities and the expert knows exactly how it should be done. Gone is the magic. Gone is the spontaneity. Gone is the mistake that often becomes the best art."

"The label thing is dangerous, because when you think you're a 'whatever-your-label-is,' then you have to be a 'whatever' expert. And when you're an expert, there's no room for error. There's no chance for discovery..."

I am still learning and still experimenting, although I've been hand-coloring fabric for many years now. As in every creative action, one idea, one breakthrough or an "Ah ha!" experience leads inevitably to another. Of course there are times when I think I'll have no new ideas, no new challenges, and that this is as far as I can go. A moment, an hour, a day later some new thought will come. "I wonder what would happen if I…" and a different direction presents itself.

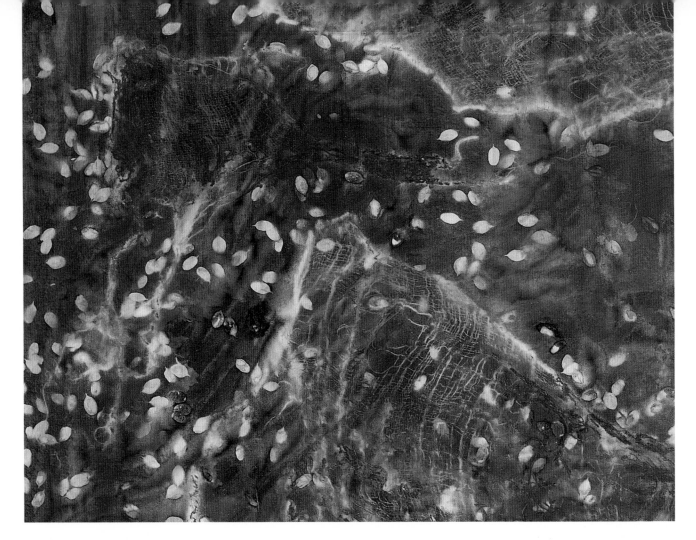

Accidental Artistry

When applying paints to fabric was new to me, it was very important that I learn to control the medium, making the paints do just what I wanted them to do. As you can imagine, half my days were spent in frustration. Yet the excitement of learning from each piece generated the next and the next and the next. Eventually I recognized where I had some control and where I simply had to relinquish control.

One afternoon several years ago in late May, I applied paint and cheesecloth to the fabric shown above, a time-consuming process, but one that I knew would result in a gorgeous piece. About halfway through the drying time, a strong breeze came up, and, in dismay, I watched the blossoms of a nearby Japanese crab apple tree sprinkle down onto the fabric. Thinking all my hard work had been destroyed, I dejectedly let the fabric continue to dry, then removed each petal. To my surprise, the finished piece was delightful. Every year afterward, during the last week of May, has found me shaking that poor tree until petals have rained down upon countless yards of fabric.

After a time, relinquishing control became far more appealing, and I would find myself totally involved in wild exercises of throwing paint, splashing paint, or scrumbling odd paint-laden materials into the cloth. Still, the results were haphazard. That's when the third option began to emerge. In contemporary terms, I guess we would call this the union of the right and left brain functions. By this time, after years of practice and familiarity with paint on fabric, the process was, and still is, in perfect balance: work that seems like play, the assurance that the uncontrollable and the controllable perform in harmony.

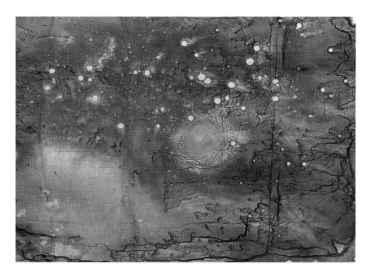

At the end of a class in which I had demonstrated an evening sky with moon and stars, I rolled up the still damp painting, took it home, and forgot about it. Several months later I discovered the piece and found the colors had moved to form shooting stars and a ring around the moon. It had also taken on exciting lines and textures from the plastic.

In this seascape, I intended a simple island against a soft sunset, but didn't realize that a small area of sky was still a bit damp when I began painting the island.

Misjudging the weather, I had painted sunset colors on this fabric outdoors only to have a rainstorm come along and wash off some of the paint that hadn't yet set. I love the mottled texture and unusual landscape effect that was created.

The paints in this nighttime landscape moved in interesting directions and blendings to impart a surreal, other-worldly effect.

At this point in time, I find on my very best days, I can predict about 80% of the final results. The other 20%, the unknown, is still the most exciting and lively part of my work. As you move through the exercises in this book, try not to judge your own results too harshly. Almost any painted fabric is useful and useable in the right quilt.

I hope you will find this book instructional and straightforward. For the most part, the easiest painting exercises in the book are those that appear first, and the most difficult are the last, the landscapes. All the general information is in the following section, "Getting Started," so be sure to read that before you begin the projects. Rather than constantly repeating formulas for mixing colors, I've included color charts for reference. Use these when you embark on any of the exercises.

For the most part, the easiest painting exercises in the book are those that appear first, and the most difficult are last, the landscapes.

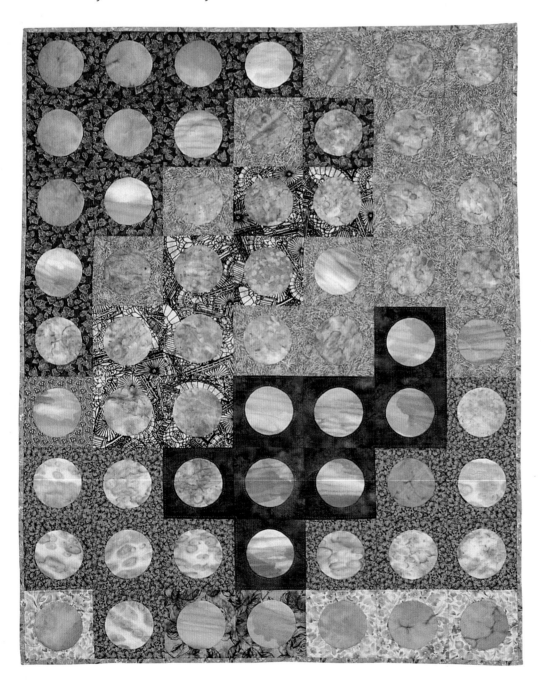

Monetones, 53" x 41⅛", 1997, Christine R. Bagley, Middletown, Rhode Island

Chris uses small circles, carefully chosen from some painted landscape fabrics, in her quilt *Monetones.* (Photos by Judy Smith-Kressley)

Getting Started

Fabric

White 100% cotton is the best choice for fabric painting; however, this is a broad requirement. While there are many types and qualities of white 100% cotton, I prefer a tightly woven fine cotton such as pima broadcloth. Because the threads are closer together, paint remains on the surface rather than leaking through. The finer threads of the exquisite Italian pima or Egyptian cottons don't interrupt the flow of paint, so the design element created by the paint is more visible than the threads in the fabric. Roaming the fabric district of New York or other large cities can offer you some impressive finds, but any shop that carries high-quality fabrics will have these.

Common muslin and printcloth, which is used for most commercially printed fabrics for the quilt market, are made of loosely woven coarser threads. The problem with a loosely-woven fabric is that the paint seeps through before it has a chance to dry. Often the result is a loss of color intensity. Muslin generally contains coarser threads as well, so the threads' crisscross woven pattern is so visible that it becomes a part of the final design, often detracting from the painted design.

You don't really need to prewash most fabrics before you paint. A good test is to dip your fingertips in water then shake them on the cloth. If the water sinks in immediately, your fabric is ready to paint! If the water beads up on the surface then eventually sinks in, you will need to prewash. But if the water beads up and takes forever to sink in, if at all, avoid the fabric altogether. The only way to get this fabric to take paint will be to literally push the paint into the surface with a stiff brush. (I have to say, though, that I have done this with an incredibly wonderful white jacquard.) It does not mean, however, that you can't paint the fabric, but you may have to brush or sponge with a little more energy to force the paint onto the threads. Often a finish can be washed away with Synthropol®, but I find it much easier to avoid these fabrics altogether. Choose white cloth to get the most accurate color of the finished piece. If you choose an off-white or unbleached fabric, remember that it is really a very, very light shade of brown and will "tone down" your paint colors. There are times, of course, when this will be just what you want.

Some silks will also work very nicely. I prefer a 10 momme habotai (also known as China silk), silk broadcloth, or silk charmeuse.

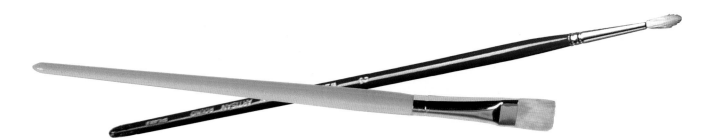

Detail of *The Lazarus Forest*

The Lazarus Forest,
33" x 38¼", 1997,
Ricky Tims, St. Louis,
Missouri

Ricky created his entire
quilt from 10 momme
silk habotai (also known
as China Silk) that I
painted in the same
manner as cotton.
(Photos by Judy Smith-
Kressley)

Anything that holds paint is a candidate for some special application or effect: paint rollers, dish mops, squeeze bottles, and spray bottles. My daughter Terry uses feather dusters to create grass-like designs with opaque and metallic paints.

It is essential that you try out color mixtures and combinations of the paints before applying them to your work.

Applicators

I like natural bristle and sponge brushes in different sizes. These hold larger amounts of paint than nylon brushes, and the sponge brushes are inexpensive to replace. You don't need natural bristle brushes of artist's quality, just the hardware store variety. Because they hold so much paint, two of my favorite styles of brushes, however, are from art supply stores (still inexpensive)—a hake brush and a bamboo brush. Both are often used in Chinese watercolor or brush painting.

Play with various styles of sponges to see the different effects each gives. Household sponges with large holes make a wonderful mottled design; large round natural sponges are great for clouds, while tiny sponges may be the perfect thing for rocks on the beach.

Supplies

A good plant misting bottle. The large styles with air pump handles and settings from fine mist to jet spray are terrific. The simple thumb-lever action relieves your hand from all that tiresome squeezing motion. I prefer a half-gallon size—big enough to spray many pieces of fabric without refilling.

A pitcher of clear water close by to dilute paints or rinse brushes.

Rubber gloves. I like the 100-to-a-box thin latex kind that doctors use, and I buy the large size so I can often use one pair several times. The non-sterile variety is generally less expensive.

Plastic containers for mixing paints. Accumulate a good selection of deli cartons, microwave dinner trays, plastic cups, or recycled yogurt containers. In our house it's ricotta cheese containers. Especially useful are those flat plastic containers from salad bars because a large sponge just won't fit in a plastic cup.

Paper towels for obvious reasons.

A test cloth is an extra piece of the same cloth you will use for painting. It is essential that you try out the color mixtures and combinations of the paints before applying them to your work. After a bit of practice, you will be able to discern quickly whether the paint is too thick or too watery, whether the colors are too bright or too muted, and, most importantly, whether your selection of colors looks right together. As an added bonus,

after much use, the test cloth takes on such a complex array of colors that, in itself, it becomes a beautiful and useful piece—if, of course, you can allow yourself to cut into it.

Salt for special effects. Coarse salt (about ⅛" to ¼" in diameter) seems to work well because it is large enough to absorb a fair amount of moisture without becoming saturated too quickly. This is the type of salt generally used in salt grinders, for big pretzels, or for making ice cream. Smaller grains of salt, such as coarse kosher salt, may work well if the fabric doesn't take too long to dry. The effects salt creates on paints are very unpredictable and dependent entirely on the amount of moisture, not only on the cloth, but also in the air on any given day. Too much moisture on the cloth or too slow a drying time on a humid day

can turn the whole piece into a crusty mess. But when all the elements are just right, the results can be spectacular.

Foamcore is a rigid, lightweight board that provides a firm surface for painting. You'll find it is available in several sizes at art supply stores. A manageable size is 20" x 30".

Contact paper to cover foamcore. It is vinyl-coated, self-adhesive, and makes a slick, replaceable surface on which to paint fabric. It is readily available at most hardware stores under different brand names such as Con-Tact®, Magic Paper™, and Grid Grip™.

Items for sunprints: rug grippers, cheesecloth, pressed leaves, and flowers, etc. (See page 71 for more on sunprints.)

Still Life with Chair, 34" x 26", 1997, Elaine Cominos Hickey, Natick, Massachusetts

Salt-effect fabric was used on the floor and wall of *Still Life with Chair*. Elaine conveys a real feeling of texture in her choice of fabrics throughout this quilt and chose an "earth-style" fabric, page 57, for the wood of her chair. (Photos by Judy Smith-Kressley)

Detail of *Still Life with Chair*

The center panel was lightly misted. The left panel was heavily misted, resulting in a washed out version. The right panel was not misted at all, resulting in deep colors but without much flow from color to color.

General Directions

It is important not to confuse paints with dyes. It may help to think of the process of applying paints to fabric as being similar to watercolor, only you'll be working on cloth instead of paper. Visualize some paint squeezed from a tube of watercolor. If you add a lot of water to the paint, the color becomes much lighter. If you add water to the paper (or cloth) as well as to the paint, the color becomes lighter still. Like watercolors, fabric paints are transparent and cannot entirely cover over any colors or designs underneath. Before you begin any of the painting projects, read the following general explanations, which will help you understand further the fabric painting process.

Lightly mist each piece of fabric just before you apply the paints unless the project directions state otherwise. This allows the paints to blend with one another so one color can flow into the next for a soft watercolor look.

It is impossible to calculate how much water to use to achieve a certain effect. You will need to experiment in your own environment until you find just the right balance of water to paint. If your climate is hot and dry, you may need to mist continually as you apply paint just to keep the fabric damp. On the other hand, if you live in a humid region, a light misting will go a long way. If the fabric is too dry, the paints won't blend into each other. If the fabric becomes too wet, the colors may fade out. Sometimes, here, you can compensate by adding less water to the paints. Take heart: in a short while you will get a feel for how much misting you want.

Work quickly so the fabric doesn't have a chance to dry before you finish painting. Allow the fabric to **dry in place** on a flat surface. With the foamcore as a base, it's easy to move the entire work to an out-of-the-way location, or even take it outdoors to dry in the sun. Having several pieces of foamcore allows you to continue working on new paintings while others are drying.

Iron the dry painted fabric to set the colors. Use a cotton setting for cotton, silk setting for silk, etc. Just moving the iron slowly across the fabric and back again seems to be sufficient for setting Setacolor® paints. If you are a bit nervous at first, you may wish to iron the wrong side or use a press cloth. Ironing makes the colors quite lightfast and washfast. I find that they are not terribly rub-fast and can dull a bit with abrasion. For this reason, if you wash the finished fabrics, avoid putting them in a clothes dryer.

Mix colors listed for each project by referring to the Mixing Charts on pages 26 and 29. Colors don't need to be exact. For example, if a project calls for golden yellow, find a golden yellow on the Mixing Chart and combine paints that result in a golden yellow. Of course, a little more of "this" and a little less of "that" will change the resulting color. Don't worry; usually anything within the range will work. Remember always to test your colors together on a test cloth to see if the combination is pleasing to you.

Beware: Paints will almost never wash off clothes, sneakers, carpets, or other textile or porous surfaces. If you must put plastic drop cloths on the floor, watch your footing; they tend to be slippery little devils!

I love using pearlescent paints in my work and almost always add some of these shimmery soft metallics directly to one or more of my colors while mixing. I tend to add gold only to greens, yellows, and oranges. Gold, obviously, has a slightly yellowish tinge to it, that makes reds more orange, blues more green, and so forth. On the other hand, I can use pearl with any color. Pearl is basically a somewhat opaque, metallic white. When added to any color, pearl not only contributes sparkle but also lightens a color. The more pearl you add the more pastel the color becomes.

Preparation

First, find a level surface; your kitchen table will work just fine if painted fabric can be left to dry for several hours, or use a table outside if the weather is warm. Cover the table with a plastic drop cloth to prevent too much clean-up later. Painting fabric is generally not as messy as dyeing or marbling, and paints can be washed off any hard surface with soap and water.

Next, cover the foamcore board with contact paper. Since it is vinyl-coated, contact paper can be washed off between paintings and, eventually, easily replaced. Foamcore gives you a lightweight, firm surface if you should decide to move the finished painting to an out-of-the-way place for drying. You can easily secure your fabric by pinning it to foamcore (often helpful when you realize two hands are just not enough!) Cut a few pieces of fabric in any size smaller than the foamcore. Set these aside when mixing your paints.

If you decide to place your fabric directly on a piece of plastic drop cloth, be aware that any wrinkles or creases in the plastic will show up in the finished painting. Warm air from a blow dryer will sometimes ease the plastic enough to flatten it.

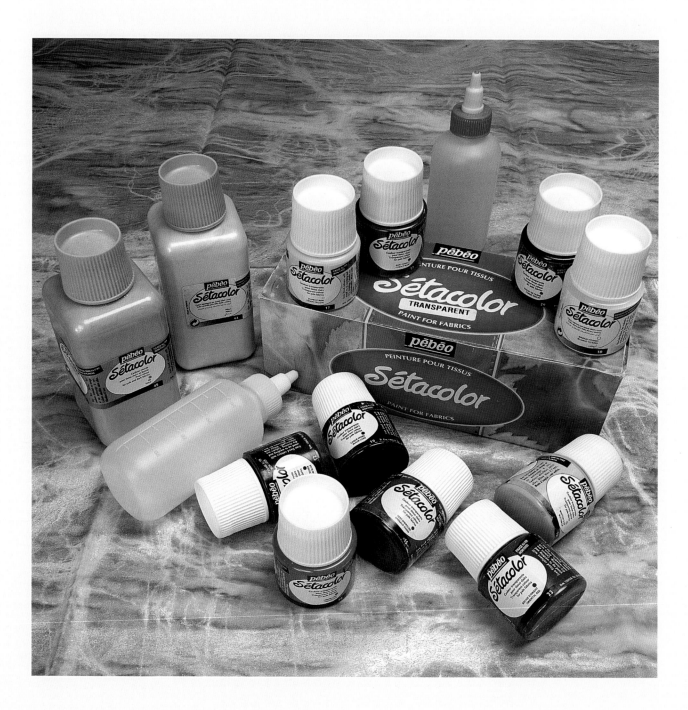

Paints

The paints I use in my own work and have used for the samples in this book are Setacolor Transparent Paints and Setacolor Pearlescent Paints. These are made by Pebeo, a French company that has produced excellent quality paints for artists for generations. I have tried many brands and occasionally incorporate some other fine paints for fabric (among them Createx™, Deka®, and Versatex™); however, since I have used Setacolor paints almost exclusively for the past twelve years, these are the ones with which I'm most familiar.

I like to dilute my paints ahead of time and to have a few extra plastic applicator bottles around for clear water. If the paints are not diluted with enough water, the result is a rubbery or sticky finish.

The Setacolor Transparent Paints work well on both cotton and silk, are permanent when dried and heat set, give a watercolor-look to the finished piece, and don't change the hand (feel) of the fabric when diluted with water. Although Setacolor Opaque Paints are also available, I prefer the Transparent Paints because of the translucent quality of the finished piece.

As the paints come from the manufacturer they are very thick, having the viscosity of honey or molasses. My first task is to create a base mixture that is more fluid and manageable. I fill an empty plastic bottle halfway with paint then top it off with water. I shake it and now have a mixture of one part water, one part paint. If you think of it as soup, this becomes my stock. From this bottle I can now pour and mix colors with greater accuracy, always adding more water to allow the colors to flow onto the fabric smoothly.

Setacolor Pearlescent Paints, lightly metallic and somewhat opaque, are great fun, and I use them in most of my work. They, too, can be diluted with water; you can choose to have just a smattering of pearl by diluting them quite a bit, or you can dilute just a little and really give your piece that "heavy metal" look.

I primarily use pearl and gold, mixing them with various transparent colors. However, there are other luscious pearlescent choices available with irresistible names like tourmaline, amethyst, and jade. My advice is to go for it and try them all! As you work, it will become clear which colors and styles are your personal favorites.

Mixing Colors

Though I am passionately drawn to all colors, the Setacolor Transparent paints I use most often are shown on the Paint Color and Mixing Chart on page 26. There are many other tempting colors available, but most can be mixed from the eight basics labeled and shown on the left and top of the chart. Keep in mind that all the colors must be diluted with water. Since there are several other good quality paints available, simply choose those that are closest to the colors on the chart.

Be patient; mixing the colors you desire often takes longer than painting the actual piece. Once you become familiar with the little idiosyncrasies of each paint color, it's easier to achieve the shades you desire.

Your test cloth is an invaluable tool. It allows you to see each color, and how the colors will look together, before you apply paint to your fabric. To get a true view of the colors, let the paints dry on the test cloth, because most paints appear lighter once dried than when first applied to cloth. A well-used test cloth often becomes an intricately arrayed and treasured fabric.

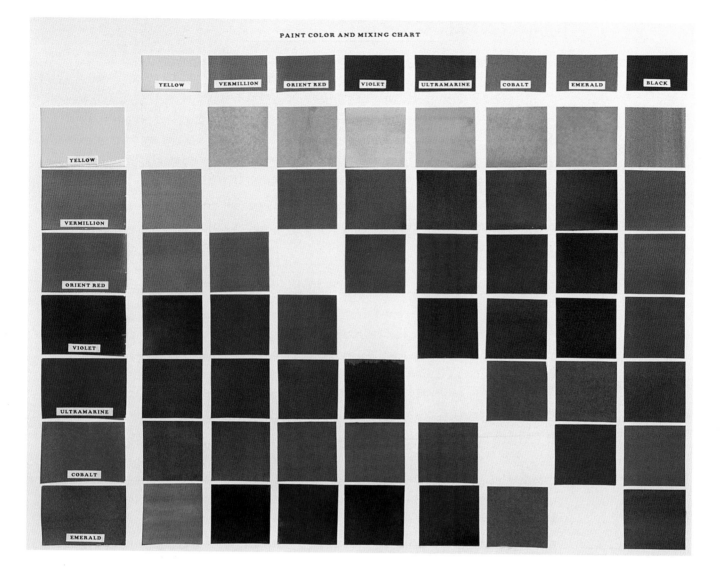

Paint Color and Mixing Chart

Each of the predominant colors on the left side of the chart was mixed with each of seven of the other colors shown on the top row so that you can see the result of combining two colors. To mix these combinations, I poured the predominant paint on the left into a container, then added a smaller amount of the mixing paint from the top row. Of course, if I had added a few more drops of one paint or the other, the resulting color would have been slightly—or even extremely—different. Additionally, adding more water will make any of the colors lighter. For example, to get a very pale golden yellow, you may want to double the ratio of water to paint.

To become familiar with the infinite variations created by mixing these eight paint colors, I would highly recommend making a similar chart of your own.

Let's take a close look at each color. Yellow is quite lemony with no hint of orange. Vermillion is an orange red while Orient red is a bluish red. To get a good "fire engine" red, the two must be mixed together in almost equal amounts. A brilliant orange is achieved by mixing vermillion and yellow. Violet has neither a dominant blue nor a red tone and easily becomes swayed to a red/purple by adding Orient red, or a blue/purple by adding cobalt or ultramarine. Ultramarine is a bright cold blue, and cobalt tends slightly toward aqua. Emerald is more a bluish than a yellowish green, so it's necessary to add yellow for a true kelly green.

To help you take a little of the guesswork out of mixing paints for projects in this book, refer to the following guide as well as the Paint Color and Mixing Chart. Unless otherwise indicated, the proportions for the following colors are approximately 50:50. For example, fire engine red is about half vermillion and half Orient red; however to obtain true black requires that only a few drops of ultramarine be added to black.

Sky: Combine pale cobalt and pale ultramarine.

Sea: The following six color suggestions will look natural for ocean or water paintings: straight ultramarine, ultramarine with drops of black, cobalt with drops of black, pale cobalt, pale gray with some pearl added, and any shade of green.

Natural Greens: Emerald with drops of black, emerald with drops of vermillion, yellow with drops of emerald, yellow and cobalt with drops of black, yellow and ultramarine with drops of vermillion. (I'm sure you'll discover many more also.)

Fire Engine Red: Combine vermillion and Orient red

Turquoise: Combine cobalt and emerald

Teal: Combine cobalt and emerald with a few drops of black

Hot Orange: Combine yellow and vermillion

Peach: Combine yellow and Orient red. You can make this as pink as you like by adding more Orient red.

True Black: Combine black with a few drops of ultramarine

True Gray: Pale version of true black

Blue Violet: Combine violet with ultramarine

Red Violet: Combine violet with Orient red

Golden Yellow: Combine yellow with a few drops of violet

Mixing colors can produce deep rich tones without the graying effects of adding black. Yet, the grayed colors on the far right side of the chart are as important to your work as the brights and the deep, rich tones.

WARM AND COOL

According to popular color theories, the warm colors are yellow, vermillion, and Orient red. Violet provides a transition from these to the cool colors of ultramarine, cobalt, and emerald. The top half of the chart is primarily warm; the bottom half is primarily cool. Even when cool colors are mixed into warm, there is still a predominance of warm tones. For example, when the very cool ultramarine is mixed into yellow, a warm spring green results. Yet when a small amount of yellow is mixed into a larger amount of ultramarine, the resulting green is definitely a cool forest.

It's important to recognize that warm and cool are relative terms. We think of blue as a cool color, but when cobalt blue is placed next to ultramarine blue we see that cobalt is slightly warmer in relation to the very cool ultramarine. Emerald is warmer still, and Orient red is considered a "cool" red. Don't get too bogged down in color temperature; many color principles become clear simply by working with them.

COMPLEMENTARY COLORS

Complementary colors are yellow and violet, red and green, and orange and blue, and, in theory, the combination of each pair of these warm and cool complements in equal amounts produce brown. If one of the complementary colors is added in a smaller proportion, its presence tones down the original color by reducing its intensity. Take a look at yellow with a few drops of its complement, violet, added. The result is a toned down or golden yellow. Combining equal amounts of the two results in the brown on the Brown and Black Mixing Chart on page 29. Of course, this is all in theory. A few drops of vermillion added to our warm blue, cobalt, tones it down. Since vermillion is not quite red and not quite orange, there is often a purplish cast to the resulting color when vermillion is mixed in equal amounts with either emerald or ultramarine. However, because the complement of purple is yellow, a few drops of yellow straightens it all out, producing a warm, rich brown.

BROWN AND BLACK MIXING CHART

Some of my favorite mixtures for earthtones, sand, tree bark, and rocks are shown on the Brown and Black Mixing Chart. Practice mixing a few browns of your own to get a feel for the differences each combination can produce. Of course, you might try to document how many drops of each color were added together for your favorite browns, but I simply can't imagine going to that extreme. Instead, keep another color chart for browns, noting only the colors you combine. After a bit of playing around, you'll be able to return to those you like.

Manufacturers make black paint by mixing pigments of many colors. From one paint company to another, there are slight differences in the amounts of each pigment. Therefore, sometimes one black will have a tendency to be slightly greenish while the black from another company may tend toward blue or brown. This is most evident when you dilute the black with water to make gray. Setacolor black tends somewhat toward brown, but when you add a few drops of ultramarine, it appears true black. Diluting this mix then produces a cool true gray. (See upper left row and upper middle row of the Brown and Black Mixing Chart.) Then again, a warm, slightly brownish gray may be just what you're striving for on any given day.

BROWN AND BLACK MIXING CHART

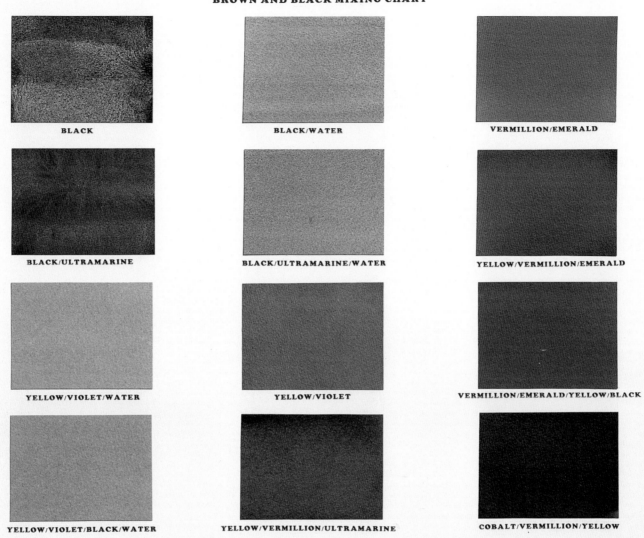

BLACK	BLACK/WATER	VERMILLION/EMERALD
BLACK/ULTRAMARINE	BLACK/ULTRAMARINE/WATER	YELLOW/VERMILLION/EMERALD
YELLOW/VIOLET/WATER	YELLOW/VIOLET	VERMILLION/EMERALD/YELLOW/BLACK
YELLOW/VIOLET/BLACK/WATER	YELLOW/VERMILLION/ULTRAMARINE	COBALT/VERMILLION/YELLOW

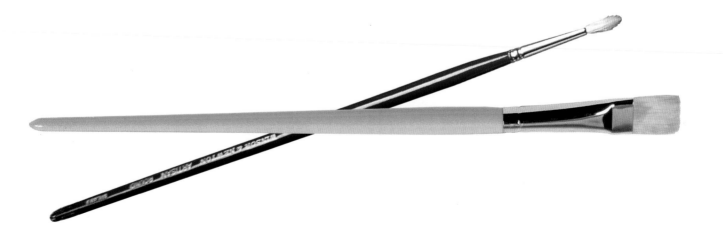

THE SKY

Of all the elements in landscape art, I find skies the most alluring. The constant variety of mood, color, and motion provides hundreds of ideas for new fabric. A short time after I began painting skies, I realized that each sky seemed to take on a life, a mood, of its own. A little more water gave a hazy afternoon look to the plain blue and white summer sky; a little less water and it became a New Mexico morning. Some stormy skies seemed to lie quietly over distant flatlands while others swirled and crashed overhead. No two paintings ever turned out the same. That's when I knew I was hooked. The possibilities are seemingly endless, and even better, I rarely have total control over the results. Studying the sky at different times of the day and year, at home in my backyard or in different parts of the country, has become an inspiring, often hypnotic, experience.

Connecticut is a place of hills, tall trees, ever-curving roads. Most of us who live here don't have distant views unless we go to the ocean. So changes in the sky seem to come upon us suddenly with unexpected and often surprising variety. One minute white cumulus clouds drift whimsically in picture-perfect blue, then almost instantly, thunderheads can boil over the tops of tall maples. A rainbow comes into hazy focus, then in minutes fades out and disappears. Subtle color changes at sunset seem to occur constantly because we just don't see them coming.

Then, there are places where the sky can be savored for hours. The first time I drove into Ohio I was overwhelmed by the amount of sky. Friends had prepared me for a long, flat, tedious drive. How very wrong! The day was unsettled, so I drove in and out of rainstorms and sunshine. Everywhere I looked, it seemed all I saw was sky: dark violet-brown rolling toward me from the horizon on my right, cornflower blue seeping into rose a hundred miles to my left. I was giddy with the abundance of sky! Alone in my car I found myself smiling, sometimes laughing out loud. When I realized that the truckers were smiling back, I became self-consciously subdued and laughed only after I had checked my rear-view mirror.

A day at the ocean or along the shores of a large lake, notebook and camera in hand, provides even more material for skyscapes. Notice the difference between a winter sunrise and a summer sunrise. Take time to really grasp the colors. Is the gray tinged with violet or perhaps green? Is that a soft mauve and a cool blue? Are the warm colors peachy pink or peachy orange?

African Sunrise 33" x 50",
1996, © Kathleen Wixted
Francis, Wayne, Pennsylvania

Notice how the pale warm
peaches in the sky recede
into the atmosphere and
emphasize the even warmer
landscape. (Photo by Judy
Smith-Kressley).

Pay attention to the feelings you may have as you look at the sky. Does the sky evoke serenity or turbulence, anxiety or a sense of well-being? Why?

Answers to all of these questions are important for assessing the kind of sky you wish to paint and the kind of sky you wish for your next quilt. Music is an essential element in my painting. From Three Dog Night to Pavarotti, Strauss waltzes to Mandy Patinkin, Harry Chapin to Gregorian Chant, music can influence what I choose to paint on any given day, or I may choose the music to reflect my colors and mood. If I come to a standstill and sink into artist's block, music never fails to re-ignite my creativity. Colors come to mind, combinations that harmoniously blend and interweave or clash in striking dissonance.

Pavarotti's *Nessun Dorma* becomes that amazing hot orange splash in a soulful sunset; Neil Diamond's "Jonathan Livingston Seagull" is transformed into a calm, ethereal sky. Together, Cheryl Wheeler and I paint cold night skies during her "Orbiting Jupiter." Brad Mehldau's jazz piano takes me to a gentler time here in my very contemporary world, and perhaps I try the colors of a neon sign on our favorite diner. But I don't want to influence you in choosing your own music. I made that mistake only once. I thought it would be a great idea to play music during my painting classes. Never again! Partway into the class I realized that, while I found my selection inspiring for painting, some of my students found it distracting, and a few downright hated it! Music is too personal a choice for someone else to make.

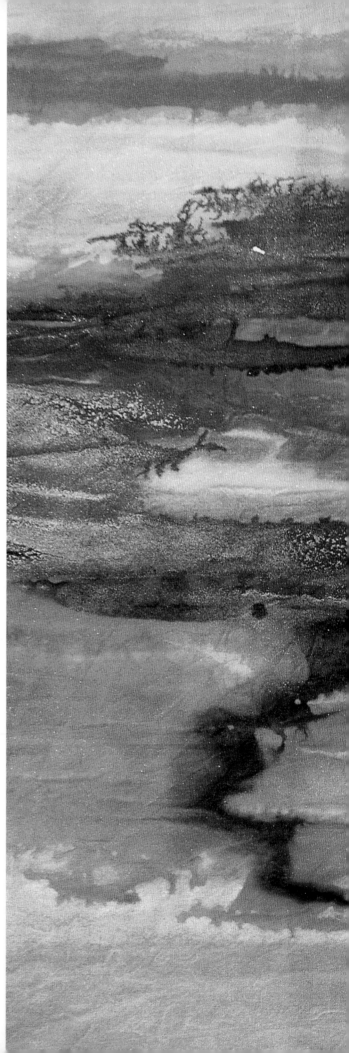

SUMMER SKY

Two different methods of painting summer skies allow you a choice of styles. The sponged sky gives a feeling of motion and cheerfulness. The other, the brushed sky, is more peaceful, painted in horizontal strokes to suggest quietude, a sky at rest.

Another hint for a successful, realistic sky is to add enough water. Dilute the paints with more water than you use for most of your other projects.

At first glance, summer skies seem to be very simple, easy projects. Yet, they often require more discipline than storms and sunsets. It's tempting to use cobalt or ultramarine straight from the bottle. After all, we reason, these are blues! But take a look at the unmixed ultramarine on the left and unmixed cobalt on the right, and you can see that neither is really a natural sky blue.

Ultramarine alone is too cold for a sky on a warm summer day. Cobalt is too aqua and gives an unnatural cartoon-like quality. Mixing the two blues together, however, results in a truer sky blue. I like to mix two separate containers. One is a mixture of more ultramarine and less cobalt, and the other is just the reverse. This gives me a slightly warm and slightly cool duo. I use the same mixtures for both the sponged sky and the brushed sky.

If the sky dries a bit too light, the finished piece is still sky-like, but if the paints are too intense, the finished piece may not look like a sky at all. Ah, but then you can always cut it up for that hydrangea quilt you were going to make!

Sponge Sky

1. Mix two containers of blues: the first is a combination of slightly more ultramarine and slightly less cobalt; the second is just the opposite, more cobalt, less ultramarine.

2. Lightly mist the fabric.

3. Dip the sponge into one blue mix and squeeze out just a bit. My favorite sponge for this project has large holes and is the size of my palm.

4. Working very quickly, lightly bounce the sponge in a random pattern over the fabric.

If you press down too hard with the sponge you'll just get solid blue blobs.

5. Move quickly to the second blue mix, and repeat Step 3 and Step 4, overlapping blues in several places.

6. Leave some white showing through to imply clouds.

Brush Sky

1. Mix ultramarine and cobalt as described on page 36.

2. Instead of misting the fabric, "draw" some horizontal lines of water on your dry fabric with an applicator bottle. In this way, some of the fabric is wet and some dry. This will give a more complex coloring because the dry area will be a darker blue than the wet area.

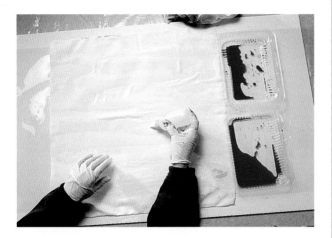

3. Next, with a sponge brush or bristle brush, apply one of the mixed blues randomly in the same horizontal motion. (Some will end up on dry fabric and some on wet fabric.)

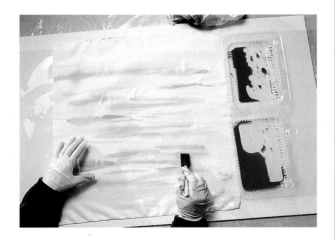

4. Repeat Step 3 with the second blue mix, making sure to leave some white areas.

Not all pieces turn out looking great for beginning painters, and the question often arises, "Can I paint over my piece once it has dried?" Certainly you can; however, because the paints are transparent, the original lines and colors will show through a second coat. For example, if you have painted yellow circles and decide to over-paint the whole piece with blue, you will still see faint circles, only now they will be slightly green. Heat setting the first painting and then adding more colors can often give exciting effects, but repeated layers of paint result in a more fragile adherence of paint since it's not bonding to cloth anymore but only to another layer of paint. This means that the top layers may dull through repeated washing or rubbing.

Wish You Were Here, 74" x 60", 1997,
from the collection of Quilt San Diego

Large sections of sunrise, sunset, and stormy sky fabrics
are used in the background of this collaborative design
and construction by Marie Fritz, Stevii Graves, Sharon
Harris, Janeene Herchold, Mary Hjalmarson, Jan Rashid,
Donna Rasmussen, Gay Sinclair, Patty B. Smith, and
Carolyn Zondler. It was made for visitors of The Museum
of San Diego History to quilt during the 1997 *Visions:
Quiltart* exhibit. (Photo by Carina Woolrich)

STORMY SKY

Storms are amazing to paint. Notice the colors other artists have used to imply the dangerous mood of a storm. It would seem at first that stormy skies are mostly blues and grays, but yellows, reds, copper, even greens contribute to the turbulent feeling depicted by fine artists. For ideas, look at some good photographs or art prints. Turn to Marc Chagall's "Paris Through the Window," as well as the art of Van Gogh and Winslow Homer. I'm drawn to the skies of Santa Fe artist, Dale TerBush. Someone once said of him that, while many artists paint the sky, TerBush paints the heavens. His skies are none that we may ever see with our mortal eyes. I did capture his influence one rare day when all the elements worked just right to produce the fabric shown on page 30.

John H. Parsons, Sr.— His Final Farewell, 33" x 27", 1998, Barbara Parsons Cartier, Enfield, Connecticut

Barbara's piece was designed and made as a tribute to her cherished grandfather who loved thunderstorms and whose gentle departure from this earth was, appropriately, amid flashes of lightning and the roll of thunder. (Photos by Judy Smith-Kressley)

Unlike the basic summer sky, where I suggested that it was safer to go for a lighter tone, a stormy sky requires some dark, moody colors. So, for this project, when in doubt, don't dilute with too much water. As always, it's essential to try out your colors on a test cloth and to make any adjustments before applying the paints.

Detail of *John H. Parsons, Sr.—His Final Farewell*

1. Referring to the Paint Color and Mixing Chart on page 26, mix the following colors:

SOFT LIGHT GRAY plus a silvery pearl metallic.

COPPER: Combine lemon yellow and vermillion to create a dazzling orange, then add cobalt blue a few drops at a time until you get copper. You may need to add a little violet if the mixture becomes a bit green. Add gold metallic to your taste.

BLUE/VIOLET: Combine equal parts of ultramarine blue and violet.

BLUE/BLACK: Combine black and ultramarine blue in about equal parts. PEARL is nice in this, too.

2. Lightly mist the fabric.

3. Disperse the soft light gray to create a cloud effect. Put this sponge aside to use again for the blue/violet and blue/black at the end.

4. Next, sponge on the copper. You may wish to use a different sponge so you don't have to wash out the previous color. Allow the copper to flow into the first color.

5. Now you can just pick up the unwashed sponge you used for the light gray and add blue/violet.

6. Last, using the same sponge add the blue/black accent clouds.

Colors are applied from lights to darks, each one overlapping the previous colors in some areas.

Remember, the color continues to spread for a while, so be careful not to overdo the blue/black. The previous lighter colors showing through these storm clouds give the sky depth and a look of an impending storm.

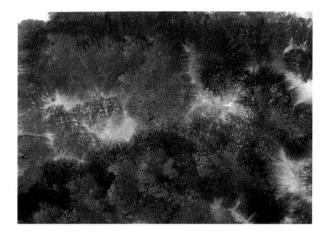

Variation

A less dangerous-looking stormy sky can be achieved by adding a few violet areas to a basic summer sky.

SUNRISE

As one who enjoys working late into the night, I do admit to seeing fewer sunrises than sunsets. So perhaps that is the reason I expect some invisible full symphony orchestra to be playing Ferde Grofe's *Grand Canyon Suite* when I actually witness the moments before daybreak and the crescendo of that spectacular event as the sun appears. Colors float on the soft sound waves of morning. Pale blues, peaches, grays, mauves, and violets are the subtle harbingers of a new day. Most of the colors in sunrise are light and require the delicate touch of watered-down paints.

1. Referring to the Paint Color and Mixing Chart on page 26, mix the following colors:

SOFT GOLDEN YELLOW
LIGHT GRAY/VIOLET
VERY LIGHT, COOL BLUE
ROSE PINK
LIGHT VIOLET
DEEPER GRAY with some PEARL added

2. As always, first test the combination of colors on a test cloth to make sure you like the way they look together, then lightly mist your fabric.

3. Streak just a few lines of the golden yellow.

4. Streak a few lines of gray/violet, allowing the edges to blend with the yellow.

5. Add light cool blue.

6. Then rose.

7. Fill in the remaining areas with violet and the deeper gray, adding a streak here and there of deeper gray through the interior of the painting as well.

8. Make sure you leave enough of the golden yellow showing to suggest the sun breaking through.

This sunrise incorporates many of the same colors used in the previous exercise, but more water was added to the paints to produce a lighter, airier effect. You might wish to try a second piece, adding water to paints left over from the previous painting.

Sailor Take Warning, 38$\frac{1}{2}$" x 48", 1997, © Judith Doenias, Forest Hills, New York

Judy's quilt was made for her husband, Jack, and inspired by painted fabrics: one piece of sunrise for the window and approximately six pieces, chopped up and sewn in tessellated churn dashes, for the background. The wonderful skewed angle and soft colors of the sunrise make the window frame appear to float in midair. (Photo by Karen Bell)

SUNSET

I've discovered that sunsets come in every combination of colors. Of course, some of these are fantasy sunsets, existing only in our mind's eye. That doesn't matter. What matters is that they imply a point in time just before, during, or just after the end of a day. Sunsets bring to mind every mood in the human condition from tranquility to turbulence, sadness to joy. I suspect I haven't lived long enough yet to know why sunsets have such a profound effect on us. I expect it's that, when we actually take a quiet moment to watch a sunset, we also take time for reflection.

Provincetown Sky,
48" x 55½", 1996,
Susan Adler, Randolph,
New Jersey

Susan's quilt exudes all the excitement of brilliant bands of skewed Log Cabin sunset colors against a soft sky background. (Photos by Judy Smith-Kressley)

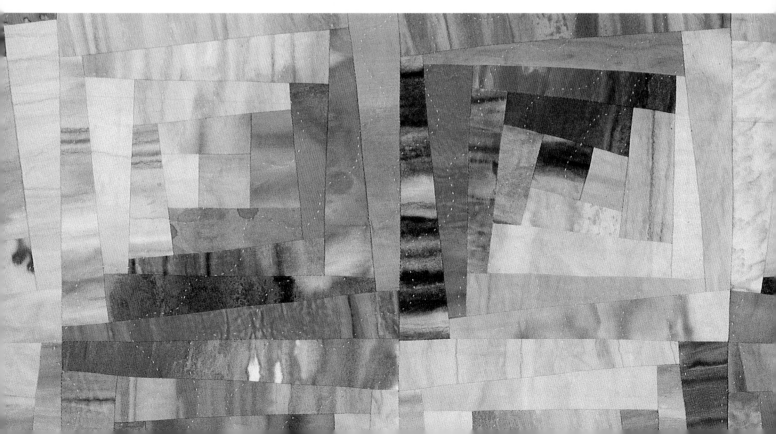

1. Referring to the Paint Color and Mixing Chart on page 26, mix the following colors:

DEEP GOLDEN YELLOW and add a bit of pearlescent gold, DEEP COPPERY ORANGE, DEEP RED, PURPLE, BLUE/VIOLET and DARK BLUE

2. Lightly mist fabric.

3. Begin with a streak of deep golden yellow.

I set aside a different brush for each color, smaller brushes where I use less of that color and larger brushes for large areas of color.

4. Add deep coppery orange, following the first streaks and allowing the orange to blend with the edges of the deep golden yellow.

5. Blend the deep red along the edges of the orange, still working in a streaking motion.

6. Move on to the purple, spreading it further into the surrounding white fabric. Notice, at this time, how the colors are beginning to seep into each other.

7. Finally, add streaks of blue/violet and dark blue for dramatic accents.

Stand back and watch as it takes on a life and flow of its own. Or, for a real lesson in trust, walk away and come back in an hour or so to see what surprises may have occurred.

Variations

In both of these
sunsets, the
warm colors are
predominant.

Shades of violets and yellows were used in almost equal proportions.

A softer, gentler look is achieved by adding more water to the paints to create lighter colors.

Heightened drama occurs by a final over-painting with a few black streaks.

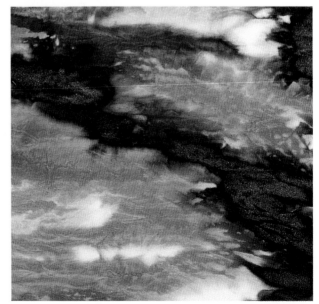

NIGHT SKY

Most of us don't really take the time to notice the colors at night, and very often there simply isn't much variety in those colors. So we have to invent the variety. Indigo blues, deep blue/violets, and blue/blacks are my choices. A streak of silvery blue or gray adds a nice touch also.

A night sky requires a delicate balance of water to paint. I like to use a bamboo watercolor brush because it holds so much paint. Just the right amount of water will allow the paints to flow without becoming sticky, while too much water, either mixed into the paints or misted onto the fabric, will result in a grayed tone instead of deep, saturated colors. Quick drying helps to retain the deep clear colors also, because the paints don't have a chance to sink into or leak through the fibers of the fabric. I prefer to dry my night sky outdoors on a sunny summer day!

1. Referring to the Paint Color and Mixing Chart on page 26, mix the following colors:

DEEP BLUE
BLUE/BLACK
DEEP BLUE/VIOLET
PLAIN PEARL mixed with a little water for spattering stars

2. Very lightly mist the fabric.

3. Paint on broad bands of deep blue.

4. Paint on broad bands of blue/black.

If the "stars" bleed out too much, wait until the sky is almost dry and try again.

5. Then deep blue/violet, and perhaps some more deep blue, covering all the white of the fabric.

6. Of course, a spattering of stars is always a welcome addition to the night sky. For a starry sky, dip a small brush into the plain pearl mix, and, tapping the brush against another brush handle, spatter the pearl lightly over the sky. Try out a small area first.

Fly High, 30½" x 40", 1997, Janice Lippincott, Blair, Nebraska

Janice's rendition of a pattern by Crystal Clear Designs displays a restful night sky with sunset colors appliquéd above the mountains. (Photos by Judy Smith-Kressley)

Detail of *Fly High*

Athough the sky carries a magical appeal, other concrete, tangible elements around us truly anchor a landscape and give it substance. Oceans and rivers, ridges of sand and rocks, mountains, a green leafy foreground, complete with irises, are all exciting to paint. Here is where we see texture, the nuances of light and shadow, where we can have even more fun with unusual techniques.

BENEATH THE SKY

The Dawn of Time/Only The Shadow Knows,
54" x 67", 1996, Linda S. Schmidt,
Dublin, California

Juxtaposed against a surreal sky, the rock
formations and foreground in *The Dawn of
Time* show the careful positioning of texture
and color to create the illusion of light,
depth, and dimension. (Photo by Sharon
Risedorph)

The Rites of Spring, 57" x 71", 1997, Linda S. Schmidt,
Dublin, California

Linda's quilt sets the richness of the forest fabrics
against the softer sky in the background.
(Photo by Sharon Risedorph)

Canyon Glow, 16½" x 26" 1997,
Jo Diggs, Portland, Maine, collection
of Lorraine Torrence.

Jo Diggs, internationally renowned for
her exquisite appliquéd landscapes,
displays her mastery of color, light,
and shadow in *Canyon Glow.* (Photo
by Jay York)

EARTH

The variety of earth-type landscape elements must number in the hundreds. Sand, rocks, cliffs, riverbeds, mud, fertile farmlands, and arid wastelands. All these have in common a preponderance of brown and gray tones. But don't let the simplicity of that statement fool you. Take a close look at the types of browns; they range from bronze through copper, taupe to chestnut with hundreds of variations along the way. Also look beyond the browns and grays in photographs, fine paintings, and pictures in magazines. Close observation reveals blues and violets in cool shadows, reds and oranges in the warm earthtones. The colors of the earth are as varied as the spectrum itself. The most straightforward approach for a beginner painter to achieve earth fabric is to mix browns and grays, but later you may want to add areas of other colors for depth and richness.

Whatever colors you choose, texture is the one unifying element to give an illusion of earth. To achieve a textural look to the fabric, manipulation is the simplest method.

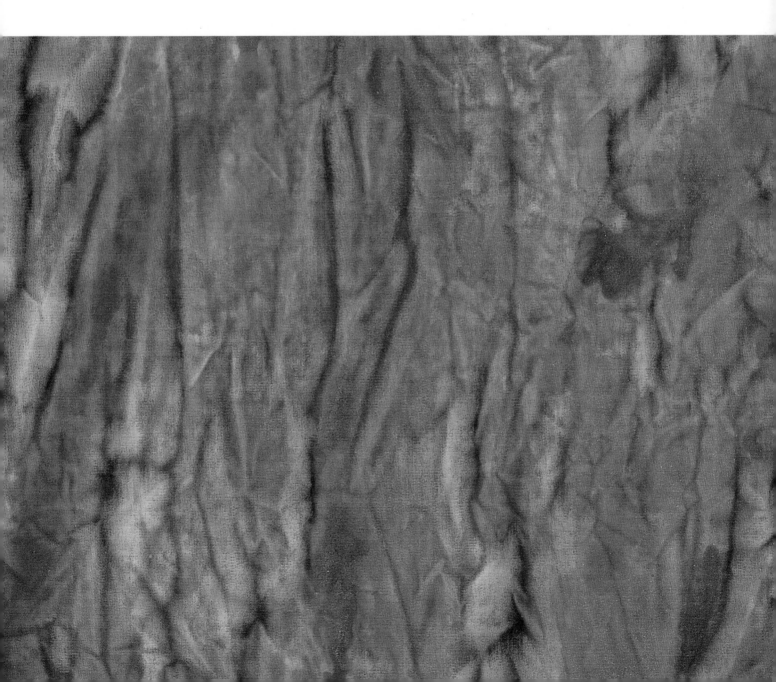

1. Select three or four of the colors from the Brown and Black Mixing Chart on page 29. I usually mix a LIGHT GOLDEN TAN, one MEDIUM and one DARK SHADE of any BROWN, and sometimes a GRAY or LIGHT BLACK. I add PEARL or GOLD to at least one of the colors for a slight shimmer.

2. Mist the fabric lightly.

3. With a large soft brush, quickly apply the colors, beginning with the lightest and ending with the darkest, allowing each color to retain some of its own space.

You'll notice that the fabric is quite saturated with color.

4. Next, manipulate the fabric, crinkling it without forming large folds.

5. Allow the fabric to dry in place. Since the fabric is crinkled, drying time will be longer. A dry, sunny day outdoors is ideal, but a warm dry area indoors will work almost as well. A hair blow-dryer will speed the drying process.

6. The finished product is a useful piece of earth-tone fabric—an aerial view of desert mountains or a close-up of crisp brown autumn leaves. It's a great fabric for tree bark, animal fur, dried mud flats—whatever your imagination sees.

Variations

The sand piece is simply a watered-down version using similar paint mixtures. Instead of "crinkling," lightly work the painted fabric into soft folds and allow it to dry.

A variety of greens with some gold and a touch of brown is an incredibly useful fabric for leaves. The crinkled lines even provide the veins of the leaves.

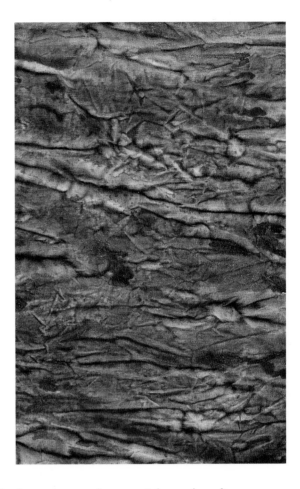

An ice or snow piece contains only soft grays, blue/grays, and pearl. When cut up it also makes great birch trees.

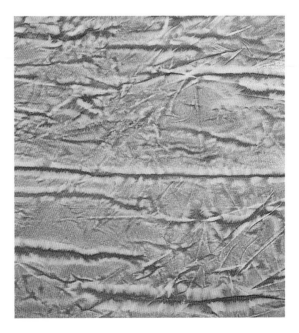

Brushing and pouring some leftover colors from my day's painting is quintessentially serendipitous. No pre-planning, no mixing or testing colors, no expectations, just letting go at the end of the day, throwing all control, caution, and paint, to the wind. I often get the most exquisite results—and sometimes not so exquisite. But almost always these unusual pieces evoke landscapes, rock formations, and geological features, real and imagined.

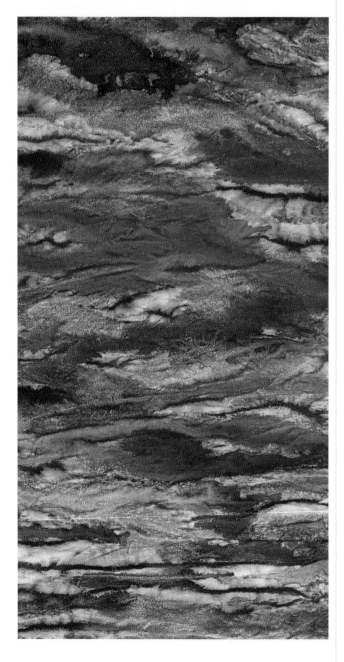

Detail of *Dunes*

Into the Wind, 33" x 42", 1995,
June A. Pease, Epsom, New Hampshire

Into the Wind was begun first in my
painting class where June completed
many of these fabrics. She followed
with my class on creating abstract
geometric landscapes and incorporated
her painted fabric in her quilt.
(Photos by Judy Smith-Kressley)

Detail of *Into the Wind*

SEA

Recently I've had a chance to vacation in a small rented house on the "elbow" of Cape Cod. Here, where land juts out into the vast ocean, the air is clean, and the breezes are fresh and constant. Sometimes a "Canadian high" will move through, bringing strong winds and choppy whitecaps. This is the north Atlantic area, and throughout my life I have been influenced by its colors. When the sky is a brilliant blue, the water, too, is that same incredible combination of ultramarine and cobalt—not too cool, not too aqua. Some days the sea is calm with no white; other days, it is shot with glistening waves. On cloudy or stormy days, steely grays and gray-greens dominate, with perhaps a line of violet here and there.

Almost always the sea has a horizontal dimension to it. Brush strokes go from side to side, skipping a bit here and there to let the white show through. Sometimes it helps me to think of my hand skimming the surface of the water, back and forth, as I stroke the paints onto the fabric. If the sky has turned to sunset, a color or two from that sunset might be reflected in the water by lightly streaking it into the white spaces. The same principles hold true for large lakes, but streams and rivers are somewhat different.

Dunes, 37" x 58", 1994

After I had painted the sand-colored fabrics, there was no doubt that they insisted on being used in a seashore quilt. For piecing *Dunes,* I also chose summer sky, water, and some garden-style fabrics. (Photos by Judy Smith-Kressley)

If you want more turbulence, such as the tumbling-over-rocks kind of water painting, a wide variety of very light blues applied on softly wrinkled, fairly wet, cloth may give that effect. Try applying the colors diagonally to let them flow through the folds.

1. Refer to page 27 and the Paint Color and Mixing Chart, page 26, for mixing some Sea colors. I mix just three colors because I know they will flow into each other, creating other subtle variations.

2. Lightly mist the cloth.

3. Apply haphazard lines of paint with a foam brush. Leave some white showing to indicate gentle waves.

4. For more motion in the water, cover the whole cloth with the various colors of paint, then manipulate a few horizontal folds.

5. Dip a clean brush into watery white pearl paint and squeeze the brush in a few places at the top of the folds.

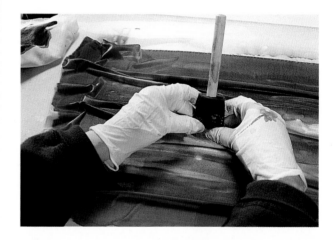

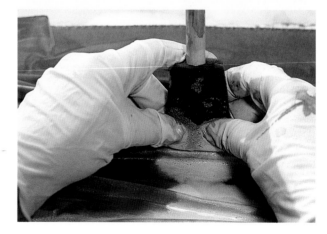

6. For even more pattern, sprinkle a bit of coarse sea salt (see page 20, Getting Started), and allow the piece to dry in place as usual.

Remember, the finished piece will almost always be lighter in color than when the paint was applied. How much lighter will depend on how much water was misted onto the cloth and how much water was used to dilute the paint. Very simply, it is the addition of water that results in a lighter finished color.

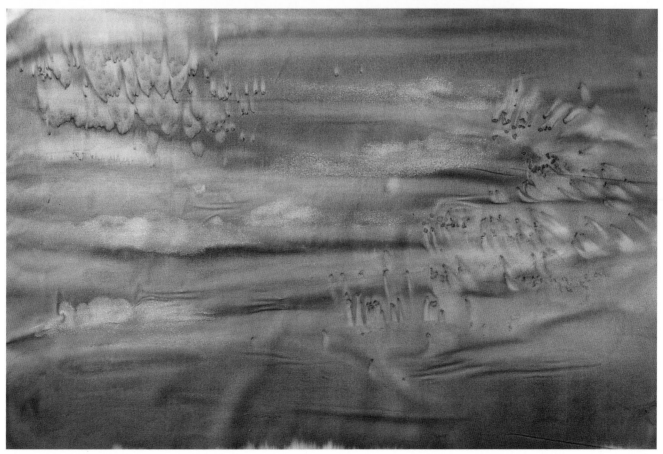

Variations

Take a look, also, at the waters in several of the landscapes on pages 86 and 87. Notice the changes in the sense of motion and in the colors.

Notice the different moods conveyed by changing the colors slightly or manipulating the fabric and allowing lines and patterns to appear.

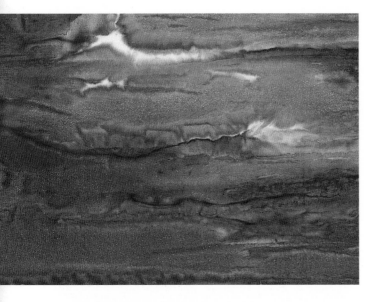

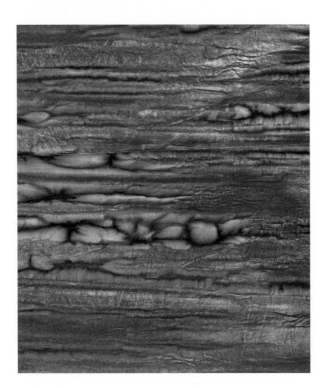

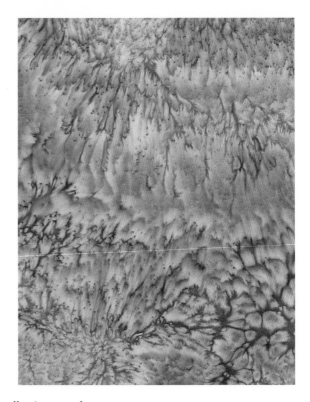

The effective use of coarse sea salt creates wave-like patterns and provides useful and beautiful pieces of fabric.

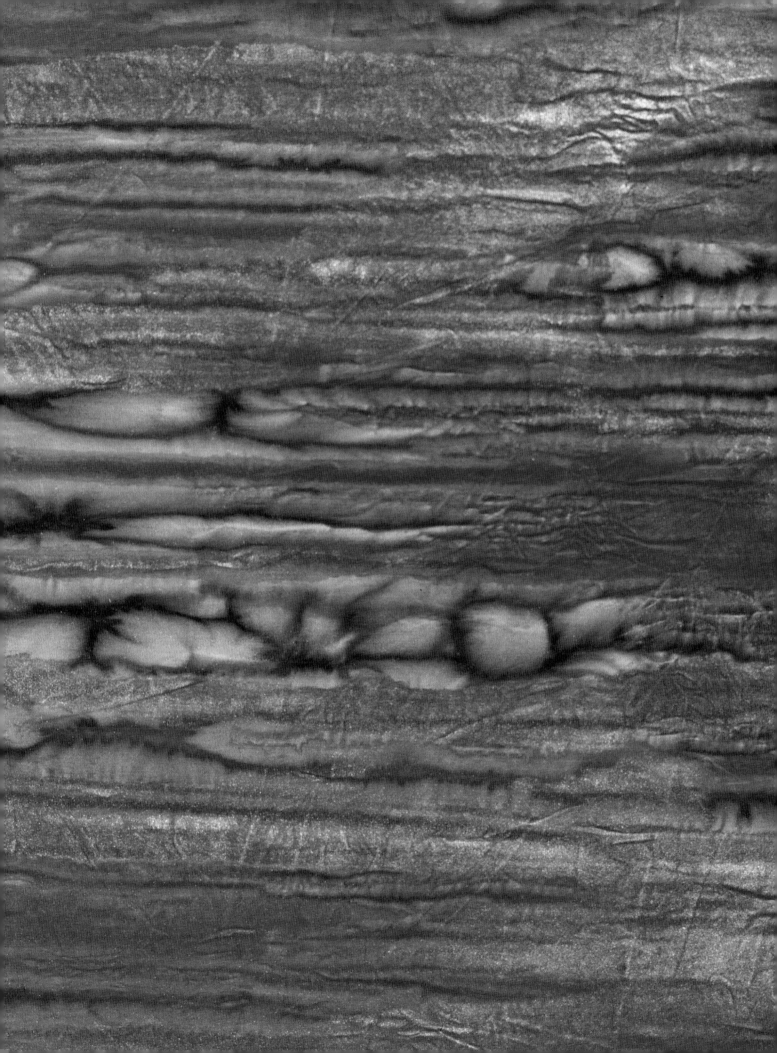

EN PLEIN AIR

As spring approaches, I count the days until about mid-May when I can move the large outdoor painting tables into our yard among my gardens. Sometimes we can press the whole family into service, usually enticing them all to come home that weekend with an offer of food and fun. We cut back branches that may have grown into the work area and put away the winter birdfeeders to discourage my feathered friends from leaving unwanted contributions on the fabric. Then we must make sure the tables are level to prevent all the paint from running off to one side. We have replaced grass with cedar mulch in most of the painting areas, so there's no mowing to be done; the mulch is easy on my feet, and it's a small matter to keep the tables level.

There is nothing to inspire a painter like an early June morning when leaves glisten in the clarity of the cool air.

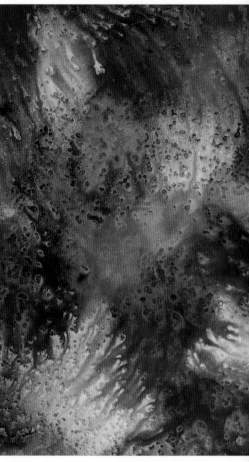

Spending very little time indoors, I happily paint here all summer until the mid-September sun drops too low to dry the fabric. There is nothing to inspire a painter like an early June morning when leaves glisten in the clarity of the cool air. I mix my colors indoors, usually during the evening. Then the next morning about 8:00 a.m. (if the weather is agreeable), I begin the day's work. I carry the fabric and a bin of mixed paints outside, wash down the tables, and stop to have breakfast on the patio while the tables dry. All is ready! Painting outdoors is by far the most enjoyable part of my work, yet it also presents a whole different set of challenges. Each of my tables has its own idio-syncrasies. One is in shade until about 10:00 a.m., so, for that table, I plan a piece that works best if the paints can flow into each other for a while, settle in, then dry quickly as the summer sun hits the paint. Another is in a very sunny, breezy location all day. Pieces painted on this table always dry quickly. And yet another begins in bright sun, but is shaded by noon. Planning is different for all the locations.

I also organize my weeks by the long-range forecast because there's weather to consider, and the only con-stant element in outdoor painting is the variables. I have unintentionally become an amateur meteorologist, each evening intently checking the patterns and flows of high and low pressure systems, calculating slight shifts in the jet stream, anxiously waiting to hear about the dew point and sun index. Windy days can raise the fabric off the tables like sails in a nor'easter. Rainy days are the time for catching up on business and corre-spondence and become a welcome break here and there.

Just so that all this doesn't sound too idyllic, there are the 95° days with 80% humidi-ty. My back aches, the bugs have found me, sweat is dripping into my eyes, I've worked in the sun for eight hours, and I'm really grumpy. But, in this part of the country, within a few days, a "Canadian high" always breaks the summer heat with pristine dry air. For these, the clearest, brightest days I plan my sunprints.

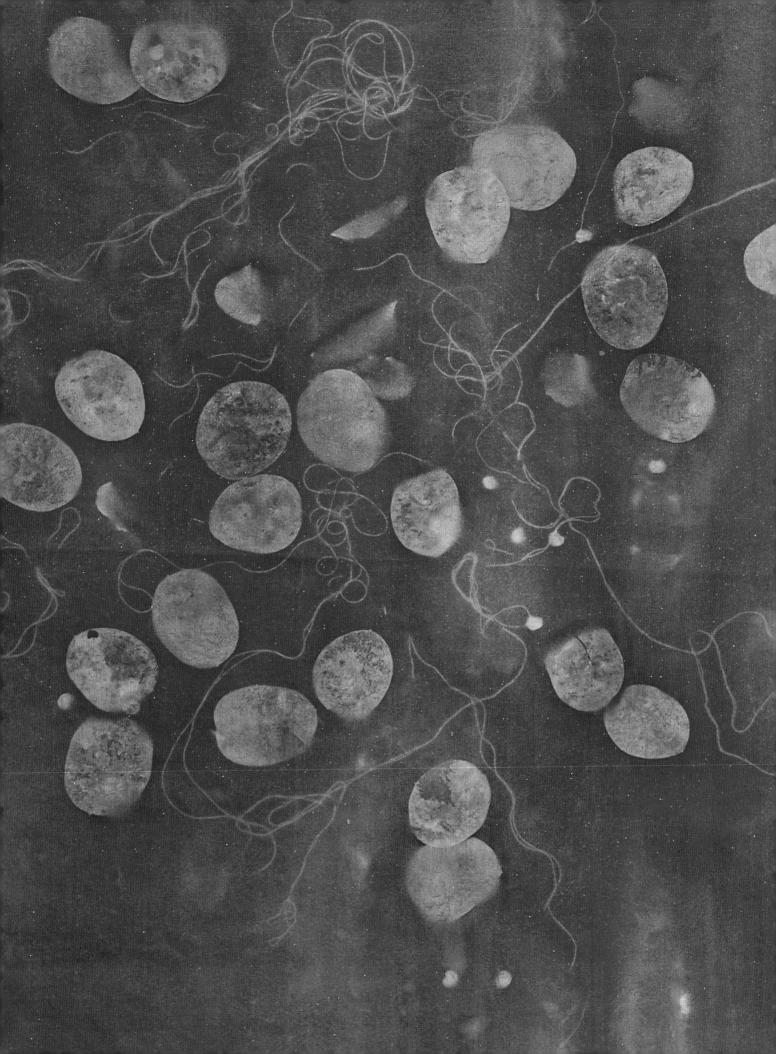

SUNPRINTS

Sunprints are achieved by first heavily applying paint to the fabric and then quickly laying various flat materials over the wet paint and letting the whole thing dry in very bright light. Because the paints are light sensitive, blocking out the light entirely with some object over a section of newly painted fabric results in a pale image of the object. The more intense the light, the crisper the resulting image. On hazy days or in most artificial light, the edges of the image tend to be soft or fuzzy. But on clear, extremely sunny days, the edges are sharply detailed. In the most intense light I have often captured even the veins in the leaves because the light has actually pierced the leaf's membranes.

There are endless possibilities for exciting effects in sunprints. Any object that will lie very flat on the painted surface is fair game for sunprints. The purpose is to block out light entirely, so soft leaves, like ferns, maple leaves, and some grasses, are good to start with. Avoid stiff leaves like laurel and evergreen needles. They generally will not lie perfectly flat. Translucent seed pods, like the "money plant" lunaria, cheesecloth, torn and pulled into amorphous shapes, clover, Queen Anne's Lace, and assorted rug grippers that have a grid pattern, are among my favorite objects to use for sunprints.

Deep, rich colors are good choices for a sunprint. Think of contrasts: a sunprint on a pastel palette, for example, will result in little contrast between the sunprint and the background colors. Deep colors, however, provide a good contrast to the pale image of the sunprint, so the print stands out against the background colors. For this sunprint I used deep shades of BLUE, GREEN, and VIOLET, then brushed a bit of PEARLESCENT GOLD over a few spots.

First I mix my paints and make sure they are ready to be applied to the fabric. Next, I gather and plan the objects for printing, lining them all up close by. Then, working very quickly, I completely cover my fabric with intense bright and dark colors so the prints will show up distinctly on the finished piece.

I immediately press each object onto the wet paint, making sure the edges are lying firmly in the paint.

Within a short time, usually 15-20 minutes, the print has "taken." Though I try to wait until the fabric is entirely dry to remove the objects, I do confess I often remove a few ahead of time just for the satisfaction of seeing the end results.

One final note: the materials used for sunprints often become so richly saturated with appealing colors that I find it is impossible to discard them. I have a large carton of used sunprint materials stashed away, and from time to time bits and pieces make their way into a collage, my version of creative doodling, when I want to take a relaxing break.

And, if all the elements have come together that day, the results can be spectacular.

GARDENS

This field is wide open! (If you'll pardon the pun.) Inspiration abounds everywhere. I planned my own gardens to surround the areas where I paint in summer and am inspired as each perennial comes into bloom. Because I am among the gardens most of each day, I find myself picking a weed here and there while the fabrics dry. How fortunate, I think, to be spending summer days participating in these two glorious tasks!

Even in winter, garden catalogues are filled with the allure of color, the promise of summer. Here is the chance to pull out all the stops, to capture the flamboyant reds and greens of climbing roses, the brilliant fuchsias of loosestrife and petunias, and to toss in some warm apricots and yellows from the nasturtiums and evening primrose.

However, you may prefer a restful spot for a June afternoon tea. Soften these colors to a Monet garden and fill your palette with pink roses, peach lilies, gentle blue forget-me-nots, and gray-green dusty miller.

Capture the flamboyant reds and greens of climbing roses, the brilliant fuchsias of loosestrife and petunias, and toss in some warm apricots and yellows from the nasturtiums and evening primrose.

1. Choose the flower and leaf colors you would like. I have chosen two GREENS, a YELLOW/GREEN and a DEEP FOREST GREEN for contrast. For the flower colors, I am using RED, BLUE/VIOLET, PURPLE, and ORANGE.

2. To mix these colors, refer to the Paint Color and Mixing Chart on page 26. If you want intense color, remember not to add too much water to the paint. As always, try out your paint mixtures on a test cloth before starting.

3. Assemble a few brushes and small sponges.

4. Very lightly mist the fabric.

5. Dab leaf colors around the fabric, leaving space for the flowers. Start with the lighter green. Remember, if the fabric is too damp or there is too much water in the paint, these first colors will keep spreading for a while.

6. Add the darker green. If you place the greens too close together, a few minutes later you may find they've taken over the "garden," and there is no room left for the flowers.

7. Begin with the red flowers, being careful not to use up all the white space.

8. Go on to paint or sponge the purple and blue/violet flowers. It's okay if the present flower colors overlap because they're all compatible and create subtle variations of one another.

9. Add the orange flowers at the end just for a little zing.

Variations

For interesting leaf and grass effects, try out a feather duster and sponges of different shapes. You'll notice I used this technique in *Dunes,* shown on page 63.

Sprinkling coarse sea salt on the wet paint can create wonderful patterns.

Mickey's Water Garden,
41" x 71" 1997,
Stan Green, Seattle,
Washington

Most of the fabrics were
first painted then sprinkled
with coarse sea salt. By
using large, uncut sections,
Stan captured the sunlight
and the horizontal flow of
water through the "scene,"
juxtaposed against the
vertical background of tree
bark and deeper colors
suggesting coolness.
(Photos by Judy Smith-
Kressley)

Detail of *Mickey's Water Garden*

Window on the Coast of Maine,
37" x 29", 1996

A rocky seascape became the
focal point of this pieced quilt,
where I also incorporated a sun-
printed "tile" fabric and quieter
textures for the window frame.
(Photos by Judy Smith-Kressley)

LANDSCAPES

Now that you have practiced all the elements of earth, sea, and sky, let's put them together in one piece. Set aside enough time for this painting because you will need to let a section dry before proceeding to the next area. The preparation time is greater as well. Paints for all three areas must be mixed ahead of time.

One of my favorites is a seascape, and it's also somewhat forgiving if the paints run from one section into another as you will see in a moment. I usually begin by mentally dividing my fabric into the areas I wish to paint. In this case, the fabric will be divided into the three following sections: sky, water, and land. A threefold division is generally pleasing to the eye, but if you decide to begin with just two areas, let's say water and sky, place the horizon line (that's where the water meets the sky) either above or below center. Doing this will make even a twofold division pleasing.

Detail of *Window on the Coast of Maine*

Waiting for the Green Flash,
54" x 66", 1997, Sue Pickering,
Derry, New Hampshire

Sue has created a beautiful
marriage of landscape and
traditional quilt design in *Waiting
for the Green Flash.* (Photo by
Judy Smith-Kressley)

Remembered Vistas, 48½" x 64½", 1997,
Jo Diggs, Portland, Maine. (Photo by
Peter Ficksman)

1. Refer to the Paint Color and Mixing Chart on page 26 and the Brown and Black Mixing Chart on page 29. Usually, the first section I paint is the water. At this point do not dampen the fabric. Mix both PALE and DARK water colors. Then mix a medium color with pearl so that the paint is fairly thick. This will be the horizon line and acts as a resist to keep paints from flowing into another area.

2. Using a small foam brush with a good edge, paint a narrow line for the horizon on the dry fabric and add a few short lines to carry the color into the body of the water. *Allow this to dry.*

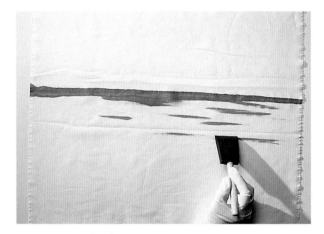

3. Next, carefully mist only the water section and apply the other water colors, being careful not to come too close to the horizon line. If you do, the paint may seep under the horizon; no problem, you now have a lake with mountains beyond. Flexibility, remember?

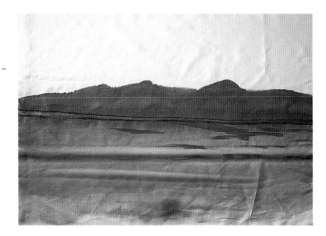

4. At the lower part of the water area, where it will meet the land, use the palest paint. This gives the illusion of shallow water and is easy to paint over when you do the shore colors.

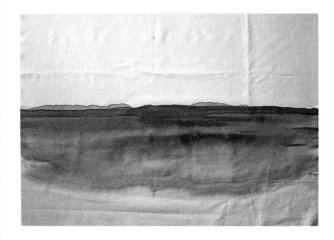

5. Now allow the water section to dry before proceeding to the sky and land. I try not to become impatient, but every so often I misjudge that very slight bit of dampness and begin to work on the other areas too soon. The results are not always disappointing, though, as you can see in this finished piece.

6. When the water section is dry, you can paint the sky and the land. Again, carefully mist only the sky section. (It may help to place a strip of plastic over the dried "water" area.)

7. I choose the palest sky color—usually a PALE GOLD if I'm doing a sunset—and brush this on just above the horizon. The dampness of the fabric will probably carry some of that color down to the horizon, but even if it doesn't, a small line of white will still look very natural. And if the pale gold seeps below the horizon it won't show as much as a more intense color would.

8. I then take some of the pale gold up into the sky, add a good ORANGE, DARK RED, some PURPLES, and BLUES.

9. The last area to paint is the land, a rather rocky shore. Obviously, this time there's no need to wait for the previously painted sky fabric to dry.

Again lightly mist and, with a brush, apply the palest color first, a SANDY TAN, close to the water line. Next, add a few DEEP GREEN strokes.

10. Finally BROWN and BLACK drops are applied with a squeeze bottle. Try not to lose the sandy tan entirely. It pulls the piece together by giving the illusion of the sunset reflecting on the shore.

Don't you love the way the purple and dark red have drifted down toward the horizon? Ah, the unplanned gifts of water and paint!

Variations

Here I applied a bit of blue among the rocky colors to create some tidal pools.

Using very pale colors and leaving white areas gives the impression of a warm and sunny summer day.

In this two-part seascape some of the lower center sky colors seeped below the horizon but only seemed to cast a shadow on the water.

For lake, hills, and sunset the same procedures apply. Notice the paler colors where the sections meet. I also added a touch of one of the pale sunset colors to the water.

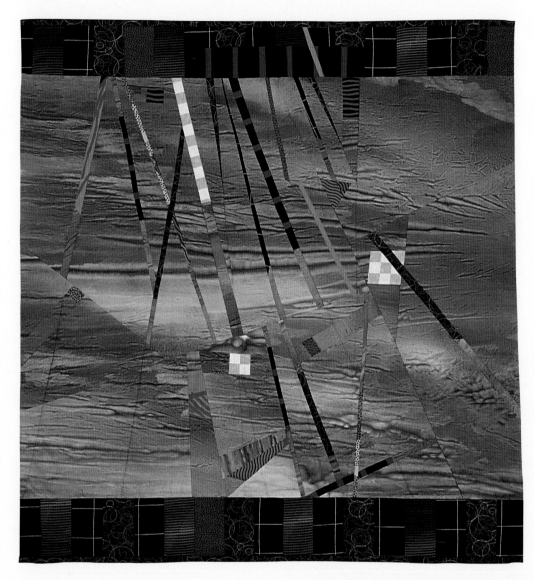

Acid Rain, 36½" x 33¼",
1997, Lorraine Torrence,
Seattle, Washington

Lorraine's *Acid Rain* splits
one fabric into pieces
that emphasize the
strong lines and angles of
the ominous strips of
"rain." (Photos by Judy
Smith-Kressley)

BEYOND THE SKY

Some fabrics simply defy categories. They are happily born of imagination, diversity, creative tension, and constant experimentation. Similarly, there are quiltmakers whose work moves far beyond the landscape, and to whom I am deeply indebted for the amazing ways in which they have used my creations, interpreting the fabrics in their own illuminating art.

Detail of *Acid Rain*

These fabrics were inspired by infrared photographs from outer space, by ancient Etruscan pottery, by tiles, and by fog. What they represent exists solely in the mind of the viewer, somewhere beyond the real world.

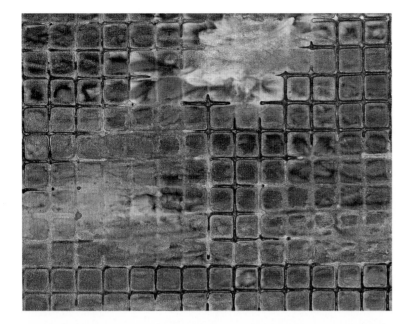

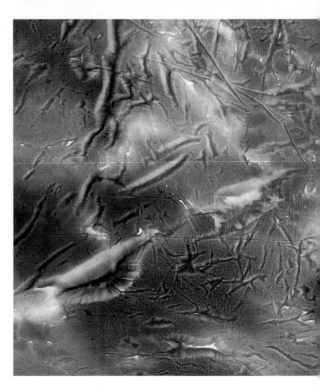

Mariner's Moons, 64" x 64",
1998, Judi Warren, Maumee, Ohio

Judi's other-worldly quilt was inspired by the
Robinson Jeffers poem *Not Man Apart*:

"It's only a little planet, but how beautiful it is,
Water that owns the North and West and South
And is all colors and never is all quiet
And the fogs are in its breath...."

Judi states that "the moons around the edge
are all colors (the twelve colors) of the
spectrum" and that the "Skydyes fabrics
suggested water, fog, clouds, mists, the night
sky, and drifting movement."
(Photo by Karen Bowers/Shoot For The Moon)

Star Map: Moon and Memory, 52" x 49½",
1998, Judi Warren, Maumee, Ohio

Star Map: Moon and Memory is a triptych that strays from
her usual table-top sized altars. Judi says, *Star Map* is "part
seascape, part beachscape, part skyscape, and partly
inspired by lines" from her own poem,

"....lost on the silver sea,
sailing a silent parallel course
lit by moon and memory."

The topmost band of the triptych was my gift to Judi the
first time I discovered the effect of Japanese crab apple
blossoms drifting down onto the fabric in springtime.
(Photos by Karen Bowers/Shoot For The Moon)

Detail of *Star Map: Moon and Memory*

Mixed Emotions, 52" x 44", 1997,
Georgia Trimper, Getzville, New York

In describing the evolution of her quilt, fiber artist
Georgia Trimper states, "I began by placing strips
of Mickey's Skydyes fabrics on a black background.
To me, the strips seemed to represent calm and
strength. At the time, however, my life was far
from calm, and so the spirals of vivid primary
colors (were) used to indicate powerful, swirling
emotions beginning to wrap around and close in."
The viewer can almost feel the heavy velvets
Georgia incorporated to emphasize the sense of
constriction surrounding the airier cottons.
(Photos by Domenic J. Licata)

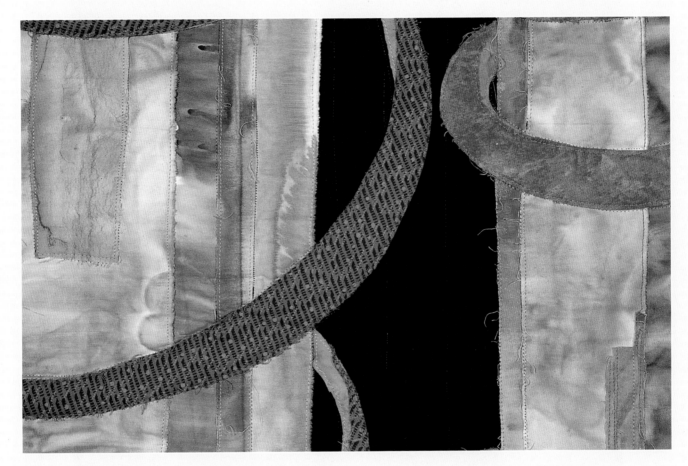

Detail of *Mixed Emotions*

Saichô/Listening to Colors, 82" x 62", 1996,
Emiko Toda Loeb, New York, New York

This piece is a striking composition of six
hand-painted cottons, along with old and
new silk and cotton. It was sewn in a
reversible log cabin construction and was
inspired by an ancient Japanese layered
kimono. (Photos by Karen Bell)

Detail of *Saichô/Listening to Colors*

Michael's Challenge

During the summer of 1997 I took on a challenge from my friend Michael James to paint fabric for a new series he was considering. These fabrics were to be a very different direction from many of the landscape effects I had developed and enjoy. Instead, they were, Michael suggested, to be "decadent, scrumbly, oxidized, rusty, radioactive, extravagant, corrosive, acidy, and electric...," adjectives that jump-started my creative juices. What resulted was a series of fabrics that stretched and excited my imagination.

A Slight Resemblance, 52.4" x 54", 1997, © Michael James, Somerset Village, Massachusetts

Some of the fabrics used in *A Slight Resemblance* were inspired by toxic colors of waste dumps, oil slicks, the natural decay of leaves and other organic matter, and the textures of scraped putty. (Photos by David Caras)

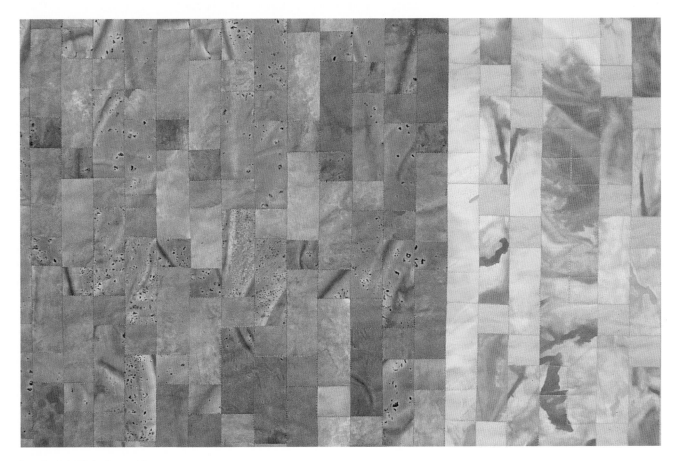

Detail of *A Slight Resemblence*

About *A Slight Resemblance, Double Crossed,* and the other quilts in this new series, Michael states that, "This reflects a move on my part to a more organic aesthetic, and offers a variegated counterpoint to the minimalist geometric compositions. These fabrics leave evidence that hints at ongoing natural processes of change and decomposition. Each of these works alludes to a world in which differing opinions and diverging points of view co-exist, sometimes uncomfortably, always dynamically."

Double Crossed, 45" x 63",
1998, © Michael James,
Somerset Village,
Massachusetts

Rusting metal and pieces
of ancient Etruscan pottery
inspired some of the
fabrics in *Double Crossed*.
(Photos by David Caras)

Detail of *Double Crossed*

Harbor, finished size: 20$\frac{1}{2}$" x 38"

(Photo by Judy Smith-Kressley)

HARBOR

Here is a suggestion for assembling some of your painted exercises into an easy abstract landscape. Though not a realistic scene, *Harbor* suggests sky, water, and wooden pilings near the docks. This project is a quick and satisfying small quilt in which to try out your newly painted fabrics.

Harbor fabric requirements:

It is wise to allow at least one-half yard of the following painted fabrics: a light sunset, a deep sunset, a sea, and an earth-type that looks like wood. Although you will not use that much fabric, a generous amount allows you to decide where you'd like to cut each piece. In addition, choose about one-quarter yard of a very light painted or solid fabric and one-quarter yard of a very dark painted or solid fabric. These could even be leftovers from your "test cloth."

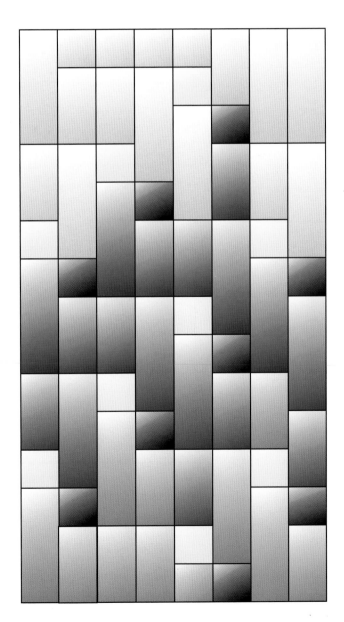

Rectangle A

Rectangle B

Square C

There are only three templates:
Rectangle A: 2½" by 5" (finished size)
Rectangle B: 2½" by 7½" (finished size)
Rectangle C: 2½" square (finished size)

The full-sized template patterns on this page
have ¼" seam allowances included.

When you lay out the templates, pay attention to the directions of any patterns to your fabric, and refer to the photo; that is, the "sea" fabric has horizontal lines, the "wood" fabric has vertical lines.

Mark and cut the following pieces:

1. Light Sunset: Cut 4 Squares, 5 of Rectangle A, and 7 of Rectangle B.

2. Deep Sunset: Cut 5 of Rectangle A and 4 of Rectangle B.

3. Sea: Cut 4 of Rectangle A and 4 of Rectangle B.

4. Wood: Cut 1 Square, 6 of Rectangle A, and 4 of Rectangle B.

5. Cut 9 Very Light Squares.

6. Cut 9 Very Dark Squares.

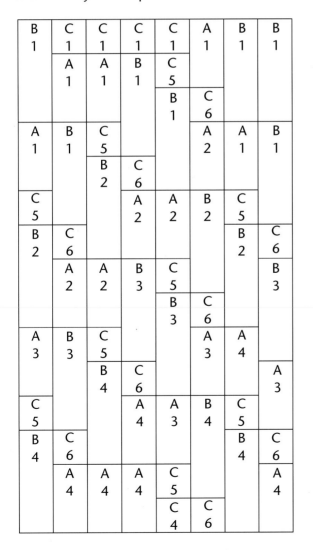

Sew vertical rows of pieces following the diagram and photo. For example: starting at the bottom of the far left-hand row, sew a Wood Rectangle B to a Very Light Square.

- Then sew that Very Light Square to a Sea Rectangle A.

- Sew that Sea Rectangle A to a Deep Sunset Rectangle B.

- Sew that Deep Sunset Rectangle B to another Very Light Square.

- Sew that Very Light Square to a Light Sunset Rectangle A.

- Last, sew that Light Sunset Rectangle A to a Light Sunset Rectangle B.

- Move onto each of the next rows, sewing the pieces together in the same manner to form eight long strips.

- Sew the strips together, side by side, matching seams where necessary.

Fabrics:

1. Light Sunset
2. Deep Sunset
3. Sea
4. Wood
5. Very Light
6. Very Dark

Pattern Pieces

A. Rectangle A
B. Rectangle B
C. Square C

Epilogue

The sky is never the limit!

Resources

FABRIC

Cotton fabrics for painting can usually be found at your local quilt shop or fabric store. They do not need to be specially prepared or scoured, just as long as there are no permanent finishes on them. To determine its suitability for accepting paints, simply sprinkle a few drops of water on the fabric; if the water sinks in immediately, the fabric will readily accept paint. This also applies to choosing silk fabric for painting.

Cotton and silk fabric already prepared for dyeing (mail and phone order):
Testfabrics, Inc.
P.O. Box 26
W. Pittstown, PA 18643
(717) 603-0432
www.testfabrics.com

A wide variety of silk fabric only (mail and phone order):
Qualin International, Inc.
P.O. Box 31145
San Francisco, CA 94131
(415) 333-8500

Hand-painted cotton (mail order):
Mickey Lawler's SKYDYES
P.O. Box 370116
West Hartford, CT 06137-0116

PAINT

Though Setacolor Transparent Paints are not often available at local art supply stores, a wide selection is available through mail and phone order:

Pro-Chemical & Dye, Inc.
P.O. Box 14
Somerset, MA 02726
1-800-2-BUY-DYE
www.prochemical.com

Dharma Trading Co.
P.O. Box 150916
San Rafael, CA 94915
1-800-542-5227
www.dharmatrading.com

ART SUPPLIES

Sponges, brushes, and foamcore board are readily available at your local art supply store or can be ordered by phone or mail through catalogs:

FLAX Art & Design
1699 Market Street
P.O. Box 7216
San Francisco, CA 94120-7216
1-800-547-7778 www.flaxart.com

ASW (Art Supply Warehouse)
5325 Departure Dr.
No. Raleigh, NC 27616-1835
1-800-995-6778 www.aswexpress.com

OTHER SUPPLIES

Foam brushes, inexpensive, natural bristle brushes, rubber gloves, contact paper, some sponges, and plant misting bottles are available at any hardware store.

Bibliography

Aronie, Nancy Slonim. *Writing From The Heart*. NY, Hyperion Press, 1998.

Gobes, Sarah, Mickey Lawler, Sheila Meyer, and Judy Robbins.*Not Just Another Quilt*. NY, Van Nostrand Reinhold, 1981

Jeffers, Robinson, *Not Man Apart,* from *Photographs of the Big Sur Coast*. Arrowood Press, Sierra Club, 1965

Index

Other Fine Books From C&T

Art & Inspirations: Ruth B. McDowell, Ruth B. McDowell

At Home with Patrick Lose: Colorful Quilted Projects, Patrick Lose

Color From the Heart: Seven Great Ways to Make Quilts with Colors You Love, Gai Perry

Curves in Motion: Quilt Designs & Techniques, Judy B. Dales

Designing the Doll: From Concept to Construction, Susanna Oroyan

Easy Pieces: Creative Color Play with Two Simple Blocks, Margaret Miller

Everything Flowers: Quilts from the Garden, Jean and Valori Wells

Exploring Machine Trapunto: New Dimensions, Hari Walner

The Fabric Makes the Quilt, Roberta Horton

Fancy Appliqué: 12 Lessons to Enhance Your Skills, Elly Sienkiewicz

Freddy's House: Brilliant Color in Quilts, Freddy Moran

Free Stuff for Crafty Kids on the Internet, Judy Heim and Gloria Hansen

Free Stuff for Quilters on the Internet, 2nd Ed., Judy Heim and Gloria Hansen

Free Stuff for Sewing Fanatics on the Internet, Judy Heim and Gloria Hansen

Free Stuff for Stitchers on the Internet, Judy Heim and Gloria Hansen

Hand Quilting with Alex Anderson: Six Projects for Hand Quilters, Alex Anderson

Heirloom Machine Quilting, Third Edition, Harriet Hargrave

Imagery on Fabric, Second Edition, Jean Ray Laury

Impressionist Palette, Gai Perry

Kaleidoscopes: Wonders of Wonder, Cozy Baker

Kaleidoscopes & Quilts, Paula Nadelstern

Mastering Quilt Marking: Marking Tools & Techniques, Choosing Stencils, Matching Borders & Corners, Pepper Cory

Michael James: Art & Inspirations, Michael James

The New England Quilt Museum Quilts: Featuring the Story of the Mill Girls, Jennifer Gilbert

On the Surface: Thread Embellishment & Fabric Manipulation, Wendy Hill

Patchwork Persuasion: Fascinating Quilts from Traditional Designs, Joen Wolfrom

The Photo Transfer Handbook: Snap It, Print It, Stitch It!, Jean Ray Laury

Piecing: Expanding the Basics, Ruth B. McDowell

Quilts for Fabric Lovers, Alex Anderson

Quilts, Quilts, and More Quilts! Diana McClun and Laura Nownes

RIVA: If Ya Wanna Look Good Honey, Your Feet Gotta Hurt..., Ruth Reynolds

Rotary Cutting with Alex Anderson: Tips, Techniques, and Projects, Alex Anderson

Scrap Quilts: The Art of Making Do, Roberta Horton

Six Color World: Color, Cloth, Quilts & Wearables, Yvonne Porcella

Start Quilting with Alex Anderson: Six Projects for First-Time Quilters, Alex Anderson

Through the Garden Gate: Quilters and Their Gardens, Jean and Valori Wells

Travels with Peaky and Spike: Doreen Speckmann's Quilting Adventures, Doreen Speckmann

The Visual Dance: Creating Spectacular Quilts, Joen Wolfrom

Women of Taste: A Collaboration Celebrating Quilt Artists and Chefs, Girls, Inc.

Yvonne Porcella: Art & Inspirations, Yvonne Porcella

For more information write for a free catalog:

C&T Publishing, Inc.
P.O. Box 1456
Lafayette, CA 94549
(800) 284-1114
http://www.ctpub.com
email: ctinfo@ctpub.com

For quilting supplies:

Cotton Patch Mail Order
3405 Hall Lane, Dept. CTB
Lafayette, CA 94549
email: cottonpa@aol.com
(800) 835-4418
(925) 283-7883

About the Author

Mickey Lawler and her SKYDYES have become synonymous with the finest individually hand-painted fabrics available to quilt and fiber artists. Her fabrics have been used as a design focus in quilts by many of today's most illustrious quiltmakers including Michael James, Judi Warren, Katie Pasquini Masopust, Jo Diggs, Ruth McDowell, Charlotte Warr Andersen, Paula Nadelstern, and many more. Mickey's own quilts have appeared as part of the "Fabric Gardens" exhibit sponsored by The Dairy Barn and as the Two of Diamonds in "Art Quilts: Playing With A Full Deck", a Smithsonian Travelling Exhibit. In addition, her fabric has been featured within quilts in many books, including Joen Wolfrom's *The Visual Dance* and Judi Warren's *Fabric Postcards.*

Using her grandmother's quilts as her only guide, Mickey began making quilts in 1970, and within ten years had constructed and hand quilted over 100 full-size and crib-size quilts and had taught quiltmaking to more than 1000 students. Along with co-authors, Sarah Gobes, Sheila Meyer, and Judy Robbins, Mickey wrote *Not Just Another Quilt,* which contained twenty original contemporary quilt designs and patterns at a time when few non-traditional patterns were available. In 1980 she opened a quilt shop and soon began dyeing, then painting, cotton to satisfy her own need for landscape and textural types of fabric. When it quickly became apparent that other quiltmakers were drawn to her fabric, Mickey sold her shop, turning her energies, and passion, to painting fabric full time. Since that time she also has been in demand as an enthusiastic instructor for teaching her serendipitous style of fabric painting.

A life-long resident of Connecticut, Mickey received her BA from The College of New Rochelle and M.Ed. from the University of Hartford and has engaged in independent art studies through university and private courses. She lives with her husband, Dan, in the town in which she grew up and where they have raised their three daughters. She continues to be inspired by the landscape of New England.